happy mondays

YOU CAN'T
UNLESS

BE GOOD
YOU LOVE IT

---

happy mondays

---

putting the pleasure back into work

R i c h a r d R e e v e s

www.yourmomentum.com
the stuff that drives you

What is momentum?

Momentum is a completely new publishing philosophy, in print and online, dedicated to giving you more of the information, inspiration and drive to enhance who you are, what you do, and how you do it.

Fusing the changing forces of work, life and technology, momentum will give you the right stuff for a brighter future and set you on the way to being all you can be.

Who needs momentum?

Momentum is for people who want to make things happen in their careers and their lives, who want to work at something they enjoy and that's worthy of their talents and their time. Momentum people have values and principles, and question who they are, what they do, and who for. Wherever they work, they want to feel proud of what they do. And they are hungry for information, stimulation, ideas and answers …

Momentum online

Visit *www.yourmomentum.com* to be part of the talent community. Here you'll find a full listing of current and future books, an archive of articles by momentum authors, sample chapters and self-assessment tools. While you're there, post your work/life questions to our momentum coaches and sign up to receive free newsletters with even more stuff to drive you.

More momentum

If you need more drive for your life, try one of these titles, all published under the momentum label:

change activist
make big things happen fast
Carmel McConnell

lead yourself
be where others will follow
Mick Cope

the big difference
life works when you choose it
Nicola Phillips

hey you!
pitch to win in an ideas economy
Will Murray

snap, crackle or stop
change your career and create your own destiny
Barbara Quinn

float you
how to capitalize on your talent
Carmel McConnell & Mick Cope

innervation
redesign yourself for a smarter future
Guy Browning

coach yourself
make real change in your life
Tony Grant & Jane Greene

from here to e
equip yourself for a career in the wired economy
Lisa Khoo

grow your personal capital
what you know, who you know and how you use it
Hilarie Owen

PEARSON EDUCATION LIMITED

Head Office
Edinburgh Gate
Harlow CM20 2JE
Tel: +44 (0)1279 623623
Fax: +44 (0)1279 431059

London Office:
128 Long Acre, London WC2E 9AN
Tel: +44 (0)20 7447 2000
Fax: +44 (0)20 7240 5771
Website: www.business-minds.com

First published in Great Britain in 2001

© Pearson Education Limited 2001

The right of Richard Reeves to be identified as Author of this work has been asserted by him in accordance with the Copyright, Designs and Patents Act 1988.

ISBN 1843 04005 0

British Library Cataloguing in Publication Data
A CIP catalogue record for this book can be obtained from the British Library.

10 9 8 7 6 5 4 3 2 1

Typeset by Northern Phototypesetting Co. Ltd, Bolton
Printed and bound in Great Britain by Biddles Ltd, Guildford and King's Lynn

Cover design by Heat
Text design by Sue Lamble

The Publishers' policy is to use paper manufactured from sustainable forests.

thank you...

to the Futures team at The Industrial Society for ideas and advice; Will Hutton for wisdom and support; Kirsten van der Lugt for organization and time-defence; Rachael Stock for enthusiasm and inspiration; Margaret and David Reeves for intellectual curiosity and love; Ian Reeves for cuttings and jokes; the *Guardian*'s Oliver Burkeman for ideas and provocation; and Erica Hauver for all of the above and pretty much everything else besides.

for MCAG

contents

contents

>>

contents

contents

preface

Happy Mondays is a book that leads with its chin. Richard Reeves is unafraid to challenge a few shibboleths and break some intellectual fine china when it comes to thinking about work. If you thought work was something problematic, difficult and what economists call a disutility, prepare to be dissuaded. Reeves thinks that human beings have always loved work, and in the economic and social structures of the twenty-first century that love is going to insist on its fullest and most complete expression yet – and be accommodated in a way that up until now has been more difficult. Work is coming of age.

His thesis represents a potentially fatal threat to received opinion on left and right alike. For the right work is a disutility, something we dislike so much that our only reason for doing it is that we are paid – and our effort is directly proportional to how much of our wages we can prevent being taken away from us in taxes. Work is an economic contract and nothing must tamper with that relationship or else it will become inefficient. Wrong, wrong and wrong again, says Reeves. It is a conception that simply does not acknowledge our need for work and the pleasure that good work accords us.

The traditional left is no less economistic. It too sees work as essentially contractual, but largely in terms of power relationships in which workers are powerless and those that employ them powerful. Wrong again, says Reeves. Of course power is expressed at work, but if unions and left of centre parties believe that their only mission is to reduce the amount of time we spend at work while increasing the amount we are paid, because the real business of life is expressed in recreation, then they too are making a mistake. If we like work, we may choose to spend more time there and trade off wages against other things we look for from work – like companionship and self-realization. The easy way work is blamed for every ill from divorce to stress is lazy. How work is organized is important; but doing less of it is not the answer to the riddle of our pursuit of happiness.

If Reeves is right a large part of orthodox economics will have to be rethought, and left and right alike will have to reconceive what the core of their campaign and philosophy really means. At the Industrial Society, where Richard is a colleague and the inventive head of our Futures Domain, we have always stood for the idea that good work is an essential component of the just society. Since its foundation from insisting that the workplace be equipped with the basics – hot food at lunchtime and essential hygiene – to the post-war campaign that workers should be able to enjoy music at lunchtime and even while they worked, the Society has always held Richard Reeves' conception of work at its core. We aim to make work better because we understand how fundamental it is to everybody's well-being, and we spend our time trying to establish the cultural, intellectual and organizational framework in which that will be more possible – and to develop practical propositions about how it can be done. Richard's book is another milestone in that effort. You may worry about individual details – in particular how the thesis applies to highly routinized factory work – but it is hard to disagree with the overall proposition. We love work.

Will Hutton
Chief Executive, the Industrial Society, 4 March 2001

introduction

How was your day? Don't give one of the approved answers – 'OK, I guess' or 'Well, it's just a job isn't it?' Be honest. You probably had a great day, engaged in interesting tasks with agreeable people. You like your job more than you dare admit. Maybe you don't have 'hobbies', because your work is more fascinating than any evening class. Maybe you like being at work more than being at home. You may feel more valued at work than elsewhere. Perhaps you have made most of your friends through work. Even your love-life may revolve around the office. Maybe it doesn't really feel like 'work' at all. Don't worry. You are not alone.

Working hard at a job you love does not make you a social pariah.

Working hard at a job you love does not make you a social pariah. Work is becoming more central to all our lives. Work is a provider of friends, gossip, networks, fun, creativity, purpose, comfort, belonging, identity – and even love. Work is where life is. And where the heart is. It's OK to derive more satisfaction, pleasure and pride from your labour than from your 'leisure'. There is nothing wrong with preferring to complete a work project rather than slumping in front of mindless TV soaps. Lots of us do. If you love your job, come out. Declare your affection.

If on the other hand you are stuck in a job that is, in American writer Studs Terkel's phrase, 'too small for the human spirit', don't accept it as your fate. Ignore the voices telling you that's just the way life is and you have to learn to lump it. That is not the way life is. And no one has to lump it. Would you stay with a partner who made you miserable? No. You expect better. Do the same at work. Demand more, and the chances are you'll get it.

Our attitudes to work need a radical overhaul. The popular myth is that work is wicked – that it saps our energy, steals our time and erodes our spirits. Two of the most depressing mantras of modern times capture the anti-work ethos. The worst is probably, 'I work to l.ve, I don't live to work.' The truth is that people who work to live have no kind of life. Work takes up more waking hours than any other activity. Most of us would work whether we needed the money or not. The idea that we should willingly endure dull or demeaning work for the sake of a few hours off is a crime against humanity. We are now more interested in living life than simply making a living. And a full life means fulfilling work.

Depressing phrase number two is, 'Nobody ever says on their deathbed they wish they'd spent more time in the office.' First of all, there are plenty of people who would if they were being more honest. Lots of us get more out of our work than other aspects of our lives. It's just not socially acceptable to say so, especially with doting relatives at the foot of the bed. And there are many more people who would like to say they had found work that was compelling and interesting enough for them to *want* to spend more time in the office. When asked, 'What do you most regret in your life?', four out of five retired people picked the response 'staying in a job I did not like' according to Al Gini, a writer on work issues. Our old-age regrets are not about the lovers that got away, as we nostalgically like to think. They are about the jobs that got away.

Wicked Work is not a new myth, of course. Work has been bashed for centuries – as divine curse, punishment, wage slavery, as a price to be paid for our 'leisure'. Bertrand Russell declared 70 years ago that 'a great deal of harm is being done in the modern world by belief in the virtuousness of work, and the road to happiness and prosperity lies in an organised diminution of work.'

Today, work is diagnosed as the cause of some of the worst problems of modern life – stress, divorce, heart disease, juvenile delinquency, suicide, sleeplessness, cancer, depression, lack of sex. Even the haven of the toilet has allegedly been invaded, with stress at work linked to irritable bowel syndrome. Pick up any newspaper on any day of the week and there's a good chance of finding a story linking work to one or other of society's ills: 'Working Mothers Damage Children's Education'; 'Stress at Work on the Rise'; 'Workplace Blues'; 'The Death of Career'; 'Workaholism – the new killer'; 'Overwork Drives up Divorce Rate'. And so on.

The only disease that is genuinely spreading is whingitis – a tendency to moan consistently in the face of the most wonderful developments, like an adolescent schoolgirl meeting a naked Robbie Williams in a candle-lit boudoir and complaining that the thermostat is a bit high. Some facts: Average earnings have increased by more than half in the last decade. The proportion of firms offering maternity leave in excess of the statutory minimum has quintupled. A third of firms now offer sabbaticals. Two-thirds of firms allow their staff to work from home some of the time. Four out of ten British workers declare themselves 'very satisfied' with their jobs – more than in France, Germany, Italy or Spain. The majority of us are satisfied with our working lives. A third of us say that work is the 'most important thing in our lives'. Most of us feel at least as appreciated at work as at home. Work is how we identify ourselves, where we learn and make friends. Work is our community.

It is time to call a halt to the rhetorical carpet bombing of work. It is inaccurate. The truth is that work is good. And by insisting it is bad we limit the opportunities to make it even better. People in soul-destroying jobs accept them because they are continually told that work is not supposed to be enjoyable. At the same time, the real impact of downsizing is downplayed; companies are allowed to kid themselves (and sometimes us) that if they fire somebody or push them into early retirement they are liberating them from work. They are 'letting them go'.

Like our politicians, we get the work we deserve. If we expect work to be unfulfilling, the chances are it will be. The Greek philosopher Epictetus said that 'it is not things in themselves that trouble us but our opinion of things.' The problem is not bad work, it is our bad attitude towards work. We need a new and better conversation about work, one which reflects reality. Governments, companies and trade unions remain stuck, by and large, in an anti-work rut. So it's up to us, as individuals, to make a start on shaping a new, positive consensus. We have to break the impasse. A few of us have already started:

David loves his work. He is a young assistant priest in North London. 'I love being a priest. I love the contact with a wide range of people. I love being able to give people support, often at very difficult times in their lives. I get to share people's stories, and I feel enormously privileged for that. Of course there are days when I wake up and wish I earned a bit more! But I simply cannot imagine doing anything else with my life.'

Marsha loves her work. Former special assistant to Donna Shalala, the US Health and Human Resources Secretary, she says, 'My work is an expression of who I essentially am. The values by which I live my life are the same ones I apply to my work. My jobs have allowed me to do the work that I love. I have never seen work as limiting. I get blown away by it, positively. It's a riot.'

Ramesh loves his work. An assistant accountant for Dixons, the electronics retailer, he says, 'In the last 14 years I have not had a single day off work with illness. There are some people who have a cold or sore throat and can't be bothered to go to work. The English whinge all the time about two things – weather and work. I understand about the weather; I'm from Sri Lanka! But I have never understood why about work. I love it. I love numbers. I'm very proud of what I produce – and I'm very proud of myself.'

Charlene loves her work. A senior vice-president at Fleishman–Hillard, one of the world's biggest PR agencies, she is young and ambitious. 'If people were to ask me what I do with my time, it would be work. I can't say I have a really strong hobby that uses up my time. I worry about that. Actually, I don't – I think I ought to worry about it. The truth is that my work has given me the most amazing opportunities. My work is my hobby. My work is my life.'

Sue loves her work. She has just been promoted from behind the checkouts in a Safeway supermarket to run the bakery. 'I love my job now, even though it has more responsibility. And I loved the checkouts too. Some people want to be nuclear physicists or brain surgeons; I wanted to work in Safeway. On the checkouts you get your regulars. I wear big earrings, and some of them started bringing me pairs in. They stop me on the street and say "hello". The other girls ask why I talk to the customers, but I think a job is what you make it. You get out what you put in. I'm really proud of my work.' We'll hear more from these five later.

David, Marsha, Ramesh, Charlene and Sue are honest about their relationships with their work. They are pioneers. As such, they can be subject to fierce attacks. 'There's something really creepy about people who "love" their work,' says journalist Julie Burchill. 'And really class-traitorous, too' (*Guardian*, 29 July 2000). Which class is Burchill talking about? And how are people who love their work traitors? Her view, apparently, is that progressive people are obliged to spend their working hours engaged in hateful and demeaning tasks. Burchill perfectly expresses the lazy, reactionary view of work that has condemned so many to suffer so much for so little. There is nothing admirable about sticking at a soulless task. There is nothing liberating about working to live. There is nothing cool about hating your job and doing nothing about it.

Today it is pretty much OK to love anybody or anything openly. It is OK for people to say they love their spouses. It is OK for them to say they love their same-sex partners. It is OK – encouraged, in fact, in England – for them to say they love their dogs. The one thing they can't say without fear of stigma is that they love their jobs.

Love of work is now the only love that dare not speak its name.

But it is not only OK to love our work, it is necessary, for us to have the kind of lives we want. Money is important. But in a post-materialist society we need much more. Research shows that happiness rises with income, but only up to a point. And the vast majority of people in the West are past that point. So the fact that we are getting collectively wealthier does not mean we are getting collectively happier – a source of consternation for many politicians and social commentators. But people doing work they enjoy are happy – not only at work but in other aspects of their lives too.

If we want happiness, the solution lies not in GDP growth or nuclear families. It lies in meaningful work for all of us. Terkel says work is now 'about a search … for daily meaning as well as daily bread, for recognition as well as cash, for astonishment rather than torpor; in short for a sort of life rather than a Monday through Friday sort of dying'.

Once we see work in this light, entrenched debates – in particular over working hours, the work/life divide and family breakdown – take on a completely different flavour. Work currently stands accused, for example, of sucking all the hours out of our days, for taking over our lives. And it is true that some people are working longer hours (although across the economy, there is actually a slight trend towards decreased working hours, because of an increase in part-time work). But the idea that work is being forced upon us just doesn't add up. Take the people working the longest hours, more than 60 a week. Official figures show that they are the ones with most control over their time and the ones who say they like their jobs the most. Who'd have thought it? That people who like something might do more of it than people who don't? Shocking! It never seems to occur to the critics of working hours that people might actually, er, *like* their jobs.

People who love their jobs guiltily own up to having a 'work/life problem' because they put in more hours than they are strictly required to. They don't have a problem – they are simply made to feel as if they have because of the consensus that work is bad for you. There is a wonderful cartoon of an artist snarling at his wife late at night, 'I'm not a workaholic! Lawyers and accountants are workaholics. Artists are *driven*.' The truth, of course, is that lawyers and accountants can be just as driven. And there's nothing wrong with that.

In any case, the line between 'work' and 'life' is rapidly being rubbed out. Few people want to put their work in a box neatly labelled 'nine to five'. Knowledge work can't be corseted into a standard workday. More people are working from home some of the time. And people are finding that work provides community, friendship, gossip and romance – all of the things that 'home' has traditionally supplied. We are working at home but also 'homing at work'.

We are working at home but also 'homing at work'.

There remains the argument that long hours, even if freely chosen, are wrecking families. Two-thirds of working women say that they are too tired for sex, and that their relationships suffer because of a lack of time. Commenting on these findings, *Guardian* writer Madeleine Bunting asks 'How obvious does the connection between Britain's longest working hours and highest divorce rates in Europe have to get before we start doing something about it?' (*Guardian*, 17 April 2000).

It may be that there is a connection between longer working hours and divorce. But there is no evidence that the former causes the latter. In fact, it is more likely to be the other way around. People who get divorced take their work more seriously than those in relationships, perhaps because they have to fend for themselves financially. That may make them inclined to work longer hours. It is simply nonsense to blame work for the break-up of marriages. Relationships end. When people – especially women – are economically independent they are more likely to end. But work is not to blame.

On all counts charged, work is 'Not Guilty'. It has simply become the scapegoat of choice for the chattering classes.

Work is actually one of the principal activities that defines our humanity. Through our work we discover who we are and what we might become. Albert Camus believed that 'without work, all life goes rotten'. His words have never been more true than today. It is time to give work a break. Time to stop carping about work, and start celebrating it. Kahlil Gibran said work was 'love made visible'. Let's have a bit of that spirit back.

introduction

happy mondays

momentum

chapter one
bad press

Work has had a terrible press over the years. God started the negative PR campaign by condemning Adam to live 'by the sweat of his brow'; in the beginning was the work. The ancient Greeks and Romans dismissed work as fit only for slaves and as a punishment from God. And Martin Luther, the man who put the 'P' in the Protestant work ethic, preached that work – preferably hard, monotonous, soulless work – was the entry requirement for heaven.

Charles Dickens dramatized the horrible working conditions of early industrialization. And with some cause – much of nineteenth-century work was dark, dull and dangerous. Then consumerism – the engine fuel of the twentieth century – turned work into nothing more than a means to a mortgage; 'Well, it pays the bills, doesn't it?' Work has become the wicked witch of the West.

Work has become the wicked witch of the West.

But Work is a good thing. Otherwise, why would unemployment be such a bad thing? It's time to throw off centuries of bad press. It's time to write a new headline: Work is Wonderful – Official.

Stairway to heaven: punishing work

It will take some serious spin, though, to counter the effects of centuries of negative campaigning against work. Almost 3,000 years ago, Homer decided that the fact that we had to work was a sure sign that the Gods hated humans. Hesiod speculated that the deities had deliberately hidden food underground, simply to make us dig for it.

Aristotle, a bleeding-heart liberal by the standards of his time, thought that work was a curse best performed by cursed people i.e. slaves. In ancient Rome and Greece work meant manual labour, necessary for the maintenance of life. Finer pursuits such as teaching, writing and politics didn't count as 'work'. (Aristotle even argued that sculptors should not be considered citizens, on the grounds that they worked with their hands.)

Sisyphus is the personification of the ancient attitude towards work and punishment. He was condemned for eternity to roll a large rock up a hill, only to see it roll down and have to start again. Albert Camus wrote that the gods 'had thought with some reason that there is no more dreadful punishment than futile and hopeless labour'. Ocnus's burden fits more closely with the frustrations of some modern workers. He plaited a rope endlessly, while a donkey chewed at the other end – producing endlessly to meet a never-ending demand.

Given that manual work was seen as so demeaning, it's not surprising that it was left to slaves – and in some parts of the world, still is. Even today we condemn people to 'hard labour' and describe a boss as a 'slave driver' – echoes of the history of work as punishment and enslavement.

Reg Theriault, author of *How to Tell When You're Tired*, says this speaks volumes about our subconscious attitudes to work:

The sentence of 'hard labour' was deemed the most severe, short of death, that society could administer. Using this reasoning, the vast multitudes of everyday workers all over the earth might have asked what crime they had committed.

Work, especially manual work, was seen as a necessary evil until the Middle Ages. Serfs replaced slaves; but the gloomy view of work was unchanged. Then, in Renaissance Italy, a new spirit was born. Work became the continuation of God's work and a vessel for human creativity – as re-creation. Work was welcomed in its own right for 'filling so well the slow passage of the hours', in the words of Renaissance architect Leon Battista. For a flicker of time in a fragment of European space, work was seen as craft, as an extension of the worker, as essentially human.

But the moment was short. Protestants Martin Luther and John Calvin brought Renaissance man down to earth with a bump. For them, work was the fulfilment of God's wishes (an improvement at least on the work-as-punishment line) and they insisted on it as a universal moral obligation. Rather than the 'sweat of brow' Genesis quote, they recited Proverbs 22:29. 'Seest thou a man diligent in his business? He shall stand before kings.'

But there was to be no pleasure in work; it was much too serious for that. The harder the work the better. Suffering at work was a way for people to prove their faith. Remember that Luther described marriage as a hospital to cure lust – pleasure was not top of his agenda, at home or work. The Calvinists and Lutherans did at least value manual labour, but they gave no thought to the needs or desires of the workers themselves. Whether or not the worker was satisfied was irrelevant. It was God's satisfaction that counted.

While Christianity has been historically miserable about work, other religions have adopted a more upbeat stance. Confucius said that a person who finds a job they love never works another day. The Buddha's teachings call for us to pursue a 'right livelihood' as part of our journey to inner peace. One of the defining characteristics of Buddhism's right livelihood is that it cannot cause suffering to others – a lesson sadly missed by the factory owners of industrial England, who dealt the next serious blow to work's image.

Factory fodder

Industrialization has a lot to answer for. Child labour, pollution, urban slums, and the musical version of *Oliver Twist*. But above all, the birth of the industrial economy ruptured the link between work and home. Until the factory age, most men and women worked from or near home – weaving, cooking, farming and caring for children. Suddenly they became commuters. The work/life divide appeared; and both sides of it were hard slog. The demands of the early industrial economy forced men, women and children to do dangerous, monotonous work for long hours and little reward. People worked to earn the money they needed simply to survive, usually in miserable conditions. The wage slave was born. Alan Fox, author of *The Meaning of Work*, argues that 'Victorian Britain was the arch-arena for the preaching of doctrines urging the specialisation of work in separation from other dimensions of human experience and human needs; family life, religion, friendship, aesthetic and spiritual experience.'

Work was put in a box.

The misery of factory workers prompted a series of responses: laws which gradually reduced hours, protected children and curbed the worst abuses; philosophies, such as Marxism, which dissected the process of capital accumulation and predicted its end; and compelling fiction, not least from Charles Dickens.

Conditions gradually improved. In 1918, workers were granted the central demand of the annual May Day demonstrations since 1890 – the eight-hour day. But even when the worst of factory conditions had been abolished, industrial philosophies of work continued to cast a long shadow. Industrialists like Henry Ford treated their workers well in terms of pay, hours and conditions – but still as cogs in a machine. They were just better-oiled cogs.

The height of the worker-as-cog philosophy was reached by the famed Frederick W. Taylor, an expert on efficiency who broke down tasks into their constituent parts to see where time could be saved. He gave birth to an American army of 'time and motion' men, who stalked workplaces in search of seconds to save.

The original hero of *The Principles of Scientific Management*, Taylor's bestseller, was Henry Noll, a Dutch immigrant code-named 'Schmitt' who was loading 12.5 tons of pig iron a day in his factory. Taylor reckoned he could manage 47.5 if he worked more efficiently – and so he did. (Noll was also a drunk and a womanizer and therefore a very busy man.)

Clipboard sales suddenly rocketed. Workers found themselves monitored, prodded and poked like never before. Unsurprisingly, Lenin, Hitler and Mussolini were big Taylor fans. Taylor did at least believe that workers should be paid more – but only in return for their 'co-operation', by which he meant they 'do what they are told, promptly and without asking questions or making suggestions'. Interestingly the most successful experiments he ever conducted were with young adults with severe learning disabilities.

Taylor's ideas caught hold in the unlikeliest places. Mary Pattison, a New Jersey housewife, wrote a Taylorist guide to housework. So, to make biscuits, 'Add salt and baking powder – 10 seconds. Stir and mix dry ingredients – 62 seconds.' We can only be grateful nobody applied Taylorist principles to sex handbooks. 'Unzip trousers – 8 seconds. Caress hair – 12 seconds …'

Taylor took people's work away from them. He placed maximum power in the hands of management, treating people as factory fodder.

Shop flaws

Fordism and Taylorism reduced the number of hours workers had to spend in factories but stripped the work they did there of any meaning. Before automation, they produced automatons. So workers were encouraged to find fulfilment through consumption rather than production. Ford said explicitly that one of the reasons he gave employees a shorter workday and bigger wage packets was so that they would have the time and money to buy the products of the new factories.

In place of religious zeal and Dickensian desperation came consumerism – a new and subtler assault on meaningful work. By the twentieth century, we no longer had to work to survive; but we had to work to acquire. And as the century wore on, the list of potential acquisitions grew longer.

Work was the principal casualty of the consumer revolution. There is little similarity, at first sight, between the starving factory worker working for enough soup to feed his family and the stockbroker doing his job to fund a new Porsche and fancy flat. But the difference is one of degree only. In both cases, work is simply a means to an end, a price to be paid.

In the USA, the eighteenth-century constitutional right to the 'pursuit of happiness' became conflated with the twentieth-century pursuit of things. Houses and cars got bigger and more numerous, but no one got any happier, bearing out the warning from Henry David Thoreau, that 'Americans know more about how to make a living than how to live.'

So long as work was seen as a means to an end and not a meaningful activity in its own right, consumerism had to fill the gap. Marx called this phenomenon 'commodity fetishism' – with workers existing simply as cogs in the production process and compensating themselves with the accumulation of material objects.

The pursuit of money can become an end in itself, rather than simply one of the means to a comfortable and interesting life. Work is then relegated to a supporting role; it is simply the way we meet our need for money, rather than our need for meaning, for fulfilment and growth. Nelson Rockefeller, when his net worth had just been estimated at $3 billion, confided to a friend 'I feel no sense of security. Now if I just had $4 billion …'

The idea of work as just a passport to other, supposedly more satisfactory, activities or things underpins one of the most depressing phrases of recent years 'I work to live, not live to work.' What this has meant, in practice, is that people tolerate dead-end, soulless jobs in order to spend their evenings watching TV – or 'TV staring' as Witold Rybczynski puts it – or going to the out-of-town shopping centre. There are people who say they work to live; in truth they work to *stare* and *shop*.

The leisure pass

Much of modern economics is based on a single, flawed idea. Free-market economists see it in a positive light. Karl Marx and his followers see it as the basis of capitalist exploitation. But both sides agree with the basic premise: people sacrifice their time at work in order to have time at leisure.

Adam Smith saw wages as compensation for the lack of freedom at work, as money which was needed to enjoy 'free time'. Actually Aristotle got in even earlier, arguing that while work and leisure were both necessary, 'leisure is preferable, and more of an end.' .

Work is a ransom paid for the hostage of our own time.

'The usual version of economics involves deferred satisfaction,' says Wendell Berry, the US farmer–philosopher. 'You will do something you don't like in order to later buy the opportunity to do something that you do like. This seems to me to be the wrong way to go about it. There's a lot of hatred of life involved in this …'

He's right. This division between necessary work, undertaken simply to fund other pursuits, and worthwhile, fulfilling leisure is regressive, patronizing and just plain wrong. It has poisoned centre-left politics, diverted trade unionism and justified terrible working lives. With the exception of slavery, it has done more damage to the image of work than any other development in history. Reg Theriault identifies the wrong turn:

Regarding work and leisure, people who call themselves humanist philosophers concern themselves, like trade union leaders, with a more equitable balance, that is, more leisure and less work for the worker… But none of these humanist philosophers are tending a machine. Certain forms of escapist entertainment aside, leisure in itself is worthless without direction and content, and creative work can be more fulfilling and rewarding than many kinds of leisure. What is needed, it would seem to follow, is to rethink and readjust work to this end.

Similarly, the idea of working in unfulfilling jobs during your youthful years so that you can enjoy some golf and cribbage in your dotage has to be one of the most depressing thoughts there is. 'If retirement is what you are mainly working toward, then you are living a mistake, serving out a jail term, so to speak, waiting for release,' is how Theriault puts it.

The view of work as a means to an end is a dangerously self-fulfilling prophecy. Once we have collectively decided that work is a bad thing to be endured for the good things that come after 5.00 pm, we approach work with this frame of mind. We are like people who have decided in advance that the party is going to be boring – and sure enough it is, because we make it so. The 'work to live' maxim, at first sight liberating but on closer inspection deeply conservative, traps us in an anti-work mindset that limits our horizons and impoverishes our day-to-day existence.

It wasn't always like this. Before the industrial revolution, work was undertaken in a much more haphazard and fluid way, and the lines between 'work' and 'leisure' were much less clear. It was the factory gate and clock that drove the wedge in. Other cultures, especially non-industrial ones, show us alternative views of work. Jean Liedloff, who lived for years with the Yequana tribe in the South American rainforest, was struck by differing attitudes to work when she watched some Indians and Italians carrying a canoe:

Here before me were several men engaged in a single task. Two, the Italians, were tense, frowning, losing their tempers at everything and swearing non-stop. The rest, the Indians, were having a fine time. Their were laughing at the unwieldiness of the canoe, making a game of the battle.

No one had told the Indians that what they were doing was *work* – and so they enjoyed it. Their language contains no word for 'work' in the Western sense. Joseph Campbell, a writer on culture, says that work only really begins when we stop enjoying what we are doing.

But millions of people have been tricked into work because they think it is the price they have to pay for their 'leisure'.

We spend most of our waking lives working. To waste them in bad jobs is a sin. A few years ago a man was awarded compensation for dislocating his jaw while yawning at work. The court decided that it qualified as an industrial injury because his job was so boring that yawning was inevitable. The real questions of this case are why on earth someone would stay in a job like that and why society tolerates jobs like that. It is a sure sign of how screwed-up we are about work.

Even if we buy the work-as-payment-for-leisure argument in theory, in practice it doesn't wash. People do not do boring, soul-destroying jobs, then spend their weekends in a mixture of music-making, philosophy and parascending. This is because the way we work impacts enormously on the way we play. The two are not divisible.

Pilots are much more likely to have high-octane hobbies, such as rock-climbing, than civil servants, who are keener on a game of chess. We carry our work-shaped traits into the rest of our lives. And not just because we choose jobs and hobbies that suit our personalities; the nature of our work has an ongoing influence on what we do after hours.

Sociologist Stanley Parker tracked employees over a few years of work and found that those whose jobs became more passive over time became more passive in their leisure hours (TV-watching increased considerably, for example), while workers in jobs that became more active took up more stimulating leisure pursuits.

Joanne Ciulla, author of *The Working Life, The Promise and Betrayal of Modern Work*, cites bingo as an example of the work/leisure link. Bingo is most popular among workers with low-skilled, production-line jobs. Spot the difference between bingo and factory line work:

It is played in a large hall and the players sit at tables that are organised in rows. There is a caller and a 'supervisor'. Players ... 'work' through their card, and if all goes well they get paid. The supervisor designates certain periods for refreshment. There is no skill or personal challenge in the game.

That's right – there's no difference. The link between how we work and how we play proves the falsity of the division between work and home, between labour and leisure. Rather than writing work off as bill-paying necessity, we need work that is stimulating, challenging, playful, sociable and fun. Thankfully, more and more of us are realizing this and refusing to settle for second-best jobs.

Theodore Zeldin, a prolific Oxford don, has the right manifesto for the future of work – its abolition. But not in the way anti-work campaigners have in mind:

We should abolish 'work' … By that I mean abolishing the distinction between work and leisure, one of the greatest mistakes of the last century, one that enables employers to keep workers in lousy jobs by granting them some leisure time. We should strive to be employed in such a way that we don't realise what we are doing is work (*Fast Company*, December 2000).

Zeldin throws down the challenge for work in the twenty-first century. It is indeed time to abandon the notion of work as a down-payment on life. But before we can start, all the modern myths about work will have to be exposed – the ones which continue to stereotype work as intrinsically sapping, demeaning and corrosive.

The stress myth

The latest chapter in the history of anti-work spin focuses on stress. Work, it seems, is stretching us beyond human limits, demanding punishing hours and eroding personal relationships (of which more in Chapter Six). It is stressing us out. Some US commentators argue that work is taking on some of the characteristics of a religious cult, turning previously normal people into obedient workaholic zombies with deteriorating health and imploding families. Work faces a serious charge: causing dangerous levels of stress.

Survey after survey appears to support the prosecution. Pick a number and you can probably find a survey to match. One in four British workers say they are 'highly stressed' at work, according to one poll. Another finds that nine out of ten Londoners experience stress at work (*Evening Standard*, 13 September 2000). One in ten workers are 'in despair', says the International Labour Organization.

A report from the International Labour Organization (*Guardian*, 12 October 2000) warns that stress and anxiety at work are risky. Depression is ranked second after heart disease in terms of impact on work. 'In the UK,' reports the *Guardian*, 'as many as three in 10 employees experience mental health problems,' and 'higher stress levels' are losing firms 80 million working days every year, at a cost of more than £5 billion.

Professor Cary Cooper, one of Britain's leading voices on workplace trends, warns that workplace stress is the '21st century plague'. Workaholism has been outed as the new addiction of the middle classes. The title of Diane Fassel's book, *Working Ourselves to Death*, sums up the expert consensus.

But the literature on workaholism undermines its legitimacy when it lists 'thinking about work outside working hours' and 'consistently working more than forty hours a week' as symptoms. On this basis, Archimedes, Einstein, Shakespeare, Picasso and one in four British workers were or are in the grip of the disease. It seems unlikely.

And most of the scare stories about stress are just that. Indeed, stress is now a pretty useless word. It has been distorted and expanded. It has become a catch-all description for everything from deadline pressure to an off-day. Life contains some stress and life contains work – the only question begged by the London survey is who are the 10 per cent who never experience stress at work? What kind of jobs do they have?

It is true that each survey seems to show an increase in stress levels, but it is doubtful that we have mutated from a nation of chilled-out yoga teachers to a society of screaming, semi-suicidal basket-cases in the space of a couple of decades. What has happened with stress is an overload of surveys. People get surveyed to ask how they feel about something, the results are plastered all over the papers, and then another set of people – who have read the articles – are surveyed on the same subject. It is now so well-established that anyone who is anyone is 'stressed', that every one of us will tell the clipboard-wielding pollster that, yes, we are too, before sneaking around the corner for a latte with friends.

There is no 'stress epidemic' in Britain's workplaces. Sometimes we feel stretched, or under pressure, or anxious, or busy at work, and we have fallen into the trap of labelling all these natural and positive feelings as stress. Take the London survey again, in which nine out of ten people experienced stress at work; half of them also said that they were happy at work. It is perfectly possible to be 'stressed' and happy. In fact the only people whose mental health is really being hit by work are those who are out of it; unemployment is where the highest price is paid. As a trade unionist once said 'the trouble with unemployment is you never get a day off.'

For some people, stress is used in an entirely upbeat way. As one of the participants in a Channel Four programme, *The Joy of Stress*, put it, 'it is hard work, but it's a buzz.' Most people want activity, they want challenge. It is not stress, it's a buzz.

It's true that the intensity of work has increased. More people report deadline pressure and having to work faster and harder. This is often seen as bad news, as if it would somehow be better for us if we all worked more slowly and with less effort. The legacy of work as punishment, unrewarding toil and necessary evil suffuses debates about work intensity. If work was empty drudgery, of course it would be bad news that we're putting more effort into it. But work isn't like that and every day it is becoming even less like that. Maybe people are putting more effort into work because work has become more worthwhile.

And a little pressure often goes a long way. Adrenalin fuels success. James Thurber, after having 20 stories successively rejected by the *New Yorker*, was asked by his wife one afternoon in 1927 if he wasn't 'ruining those stories by spending so much time on them'. She advised him to give himself a 45-minute time limit for his next story. Thurber did just that, sent off his piece – and received an acceptance letter in a matter of days.

Any life worth living is full of 'stresses'. A life with a wide range of choices, aspirations, paths and challenges, and with stretching and demanding work, feels more challenging than one with predictable, repetitive, dull jobs and activities, and limited horizons. And thank God for that. As Kierkegaard put it, 'Anxiety is freedom.'

This is not to say that there aren't some workplaces that damage mental health – simply that the vast majority do not. The real issue is control. As long as we feel in control of our work our psychological health is unlikely to suffer. Self-generated pressure to produce the best presentation is not stress; it is personal pride and ambition. And pride and ambition are good for you.

For many centuries work has been labelled curse, punishment, religious instruction, necessary evil, survival course, time bandit, marriage-wrecker and depressant. And the spin continues to the present day. A long list of maladies is linked to work: we are more anxious and less horny; more rushed and less homely; more sick and less polite; more addicted and less happy than ever before. And work is supposedly to blame. There is an anti-work case being put in persuasive terms on an almost daily basis. There is only one problem with it. It's bunkum. Work is simply the scapegoat. For the truth, whisper it softly, is that as far as work is concerned, we've never had it so good.

chapter two
my work, my self

The eponymous hero of *Billy Elliot* is a boy brought up in a working-class mining community who fulfils his dream to become a ballet dancer. The film has been variously described as a study in social mobility, an insight into the tensions of modern masculinity and as a morality tale about the importance of letting children go.

In fact, the film is a fairly straightforward story about work. Billy wants a different kind of work from the people around him. He wants to jump *sisonnes* rather than shovel coal. And he does. Billy wants to express himself through his work and correctly thinks he will get more out of Covent Garden than the coal mine. For him, his work represents freedom. Freedom from what John Stuart Mill called the 'despotism of custom'. Freedom to go his own way. The fact that in doing so he is the exception to the rule simply shows how badly the rule needs updating.

We are what we do.

Work and identity are inextricably bound together. Our work expresses and defines who we are. Samuel Butler wrote that 'every man's work, whether it be literature or music or pictures or architecture or anything else, is always a portrait of himself.'

And the portraiture of work is becoming even more important. With the decline of other labels, it is the new identity tag. Class, race, gender, sexuality, geography, parental status and family are all less important signifiers of who we are and what makes us tick. Geographical roots have weakened, religious affiliations have diminished and the extended family has dispersed, leaving the way we spend our labouring hours as the clearest window into our souls. We are what we do.

'Work is clearly becoming more important,' says Michael Willmott, co-director of the Future Foundation think-tank. 'People are getting at least as much sense of who they are from their work as from their family and friends.'

The fact that we can 'do a Billy' and choose our own path makes it all the more personal. Our work is a shorthand for ourselves. Who wants to say they do a job because their Dad did it? Think about the question we ask children. Not what do you want to *do* when you grow up, but what do you want to *be*? The joke is that parents are asking this because they are casting around for ideas. But for many people, discovering they have landed themselves in a career rut, asking the question again is a powerful exercise. What do I want to *be*?

The sheer volume of anti-work rhetoric has blinded us for too long to the unalterable position of work at the centre of our lives. It has delayed the voyage of exploration for work that gives our lives value, meaning and expression, for work that we can be proud of – in short, for a life's work.

David says that more people are thinking about their work in terms of a vocation – in the proper sense of the term. 'There is a view that vocation is like God rounding people up for a rehearsal for life and handing out parts. The secular equivalent is people thinking that because they have A levels in this, they should do that. But vocation is really about being true to yourself, about being more essentially human.'

Occupational psychologies

There is a *New Yorker* cartoon that depicts an unshaven man in climbing gear coming face to face with an identical man wearing a dark suit and carrying a briefcase and newspaper. 'Stanley was deeply disappointed,' the caption reads, 'when, high in the Tibetan mountains, he finally found his true self.'

The cartoon is funny because it gently mocks the fashion for adventure travel as a route to the 'inner self' and because it cruelly exposes the myth that if only we look hard enough we will discover we are not really loss-adjusters or accountants.

But Stanley should not be disappointed. He should be delighted that he has found a job which reflects the real him. Stanley is one of the lucky ones whose work expresses and defines him. He can get off the mountain and go back to his desk a happy man.

We cannot escape from the fact that work maketh the man, and of course the woman too. After all, most people spend most of their waking lives doing it. Who would deny that the relationships we have with partners over the course of our lives shape us? Yet we spend more time with our work than with our wives, husbands or lovers.

Sigmund Freud said that love and work were the two foundations of communal life, giving us 'better control over the external world'. Work, he said, gives us 'a secure place in the human community'. Having said that, Freud then went on to focus almost exclusively on love in his work (which he loved).

Work helps to define 'ego boundaries' – the lines between individuals and the rest of the world. Al Gini, paraphrasing psychiatrist Leonard Fagin, says that the 'psychopathology' of work 'not only identifies us, but it also identifies what we are not, and thus defines our role boundaries, and group and class identities'.

Maslow's famous hierarchy of needs, having covered all the basics – physical requirements, security, companionship and self-worth, peaks with 'self-actualization'. This can only be achieved with the right work: 'Even if all these [lower] needs are satisfied, we may still often (if not always) expect that a new discontent and restlessness will soon develop unless the individual is doing what he is fitted for.'

We don't go to parties and introduce ourselves by saying 'Hello, I'm Rona. I prefer the early fiction of Martin Amis,' or, 'Hi, I'm from Fenney Bentley in Derbyshire,' or, 'I support the Royal Society for the Protection of Birds, what do you do?'. There's a good reason for this. Our work is more important than any other single factor in defining who we are. It is, in Maslow's terms, how we 'actualize' ourselves.

David certainly identifies himself through his ministry. 'It defines the whole of who I am. I don't stop being a priest in the bath, or asleep, or in the pub chatting with friends. It isn't simply a group of tasks, it is a role in a community.'

Philosopher Martin Heidegger wrote that 'you are your projects.' The work that we do reflects and shapes our personalities. We continuously regenerate ourselves through our labours. Work is the primary site in which people find and create meaning in their lives; one reason why people so badly want to do it.

Benjamin Kline Hunnicut, in *Kellogg's Six-Hour Day*, records how in 1930 W. W. Kellogg cut working hours in his Battle Creek cereal factory from eight to six hours a day. This meant fewer lay-offs during the ensuing economic depression. But after World War II there was pressure – from the workers as well as management – for a return to the eight-hour day, which was duly reinstated.

Hunnicut sees this as a regressive step, because he is essentially opposed to work. But Alan Wolfe, rightly savaging the 'lack of moral imagination among the critics of work', speculates, 'They may have wanted to go back to full-time work because it was in full-time work that they found more of themselves.' (*The American Prospect*, September 1997).

The crucial part played by work in the creation of modern identities makes bad jobs – jobs in which people are treated badly, in which creativity is crushed, in which workers are seen as mere cogs in the machine – even more poisonous. They do not simply pollute the hours between clocking on and heading for home. They distort the whole of people's lives, making them less than the people they want to be.

Work is the raw material from which we construct our lives. At its worst, stupid work makes for dull people. But at its best, liberating work makes for free lives. Work can be a great healer, too. Work can help restore and maintain our sense of ourselves during the purple patches of our lives. Most people know the story of John Harrison and his clocks, which solved the puzzle of how to measure longitude, the biggest scientific problem of the eighteenth century, and his struggle to be recognized. But a lesser-known story, as told by Dava Sobel, in *Longitude*, is of Lieutenant Commander Rupert T. Gould, who restored the clocks over a twelve-year period, for no pay, from 1920 onwards.

Gould had suffered a nervous breakdown at the outset of World War I and had seen the destruction of his marriage splattered across the tabloid press, losing his naval commission in the process. Gould put the bits and pieces of his own life together as he cleaned the clocks, as Sobel writes 'By putting them back to rights, he nursed himself back to health and peace of mind.'

Women's work

The link between work and identity is no longer made through the Y chromosome. Women, who make up half the workforce in both the UK and the US, now define themselves in terms of their work rather than their status as wives or mothers. Many are choosing not to have children at all. Even those who do are reluctant to swap their status at work for the life of a housewife. Andrew Hacker points out in 'Who Needs Kids?', in the *New York Review of Books* (2000), that modern mothers of young children are working even in households where the father's income is large enough for them to stay at home. 'They want as much as men the freedoms and opportunities to be found outside the home,' he says.

Indeed, for women who are in the first generation to enjoy similar opportunities to men at work, the issue of identity is more important than for many of their male peers. The independence that work brings them is hard-won – and therefore hugely significant.

Susan Faludi, a feminist writer, points out that 'the issue of identity through work comes up at every level. For every woman, whether clerk or secretary, to them their work is important … It isn't just about the paycheck … Part of your identity is that you can support yourself and that you are part of a public world …' Women are relishing the independence offered by their own wage packets and the satisfaction offered by a fulfilling work life. The social revolution of the last few decades has glued women to work – and they have no intention of coming unstuck.

Sewers and self-esteem

All this work-as-self stuff is all very well for creative types, of course.
But what about people doing low-paid, 'undesirable' work? Surely
their work does not define them? Wrong. Take the lottery-winning
dinner lady who went back to work the next day. There is no
consistent link between occupational status and job satisfaction.
Anthropologist Judith Doyle points out that the men who work
many feet below the rest of us, in London's sewers, are strongly
defined by their work:

The sewer cleaners hinted at their sense of work as identity when they [said]
that you are not a sewer man until you've been dunked ... For council sewer
cleaners, doing the job is not enough, you must *be* a sewer man and you are
not a sewer man until you've fallen in the water.

To most middle-class commentators, sewer-cleaning seems like the
sort of job no one would want to do, or enjoy, or get a sense of
satisfaction from. There is a terrible snobbery about work among
many of the academics and journalists who write about it. They
assume it is fine for them to love their jobs, but find it impossible to
imagine that someone in a job they would personally find boring or
distasteful might enjoy their work too.

Al Gini quotes a firebrand employment lawyer on the subject.
'Dignity? Finding dignity in doing a job well? What dignity can be
found in a job task that ends with the phrase, "Would you like fries
with your order, sir?"' Actually, quite a bit. People doing low-paid
service jobs can get satisfaction from their work (indeed domestic
workers are the most satisfied occupational group in the UK) and
plenty of lawyers can find their work empty, demeaning and dull. In
a recent US survey, 83 per cent of the population said that their work
was an important part of their self-worth and in a poll by Robert

Wuthnow, professor of sociology at Princeton University, 84 per cent of full-time workers said their work was absolutely essential or very important to their sense of personal worth. Of the respondents, 82 per cent said the statement 'my work is very meaningful to me' described them very well or fairly well.

Marsha says it about attitude, not status. 'It can be a fry-stand of a McDonalds's if the people there love their work. It's about energy.'

Work and self-esteem are inextricably bound together. Not just for white-collar creatives, for all of us. Doyle asked people where they felt 'most appreciated' – at work, at home or equally at work and at home. Of her respondents, 70 per cent felt either equally appreciated in both spheres of their life or most appreciated at work. Albert Einstein once said that 'work is the only thing that gives substance to life'.

happy mondays

momentum

Work thing, you make my heart sing

When Anne Sweeney was offered the presidency of the Disney Channel, the question she asked herself was not whether the stock options were sufficient or the long-term growth forecasts aggressive enough but 'Will this job make my heart sing?' (She thought it would.)

Sweeney wanted a job that inspired and stretched her. She's not alone. With the growing importance of work to our identities, we want jobs that act as vehicles for our passions. We want our work to be an act of self-expression. David Brooks, in *Bobos in Paradise*, argues that the new elite, highly educated 'Bourgeois Bohemians', or Bobos, are in the front line of redefining work. Reconciling the values of materialism and hippy notions of exploration, they are not interested in work which just pays the bills:

For Bobos work is not boring. It's challenging and interesting … They have transformed work into a spiritual and intellectual vocation, so they approach their labour with the fervour of artists and missionaries … Their collars may not be buttoned up and their desks may not be neat, but they are, after a fashion, quite self-disciplined. Members of the educated class often regard work as an expression of their entire being, so of course they devote themselves to it with phenomenal energy. For many there is no time when they are not at work; they are always thinking.

Brooks is right. When work feels like an expression of who we are, we are likely to do more of it. Charlie Tellerman, who escaped from big corporate life to set up his own music agency, says, 'Work is so much part of my life that I don't think of it in terms of hours. I'm glad I'm doing it. I sometimes miss it at the weekends, and especially Bank Holidays. And I go to sleep early on Sundays (*Observer*, 23 July 2000).

Ramesh spends his Saturdays studying for his next accountancy qualification after spending his weekdays doing accounting. He adores it. 'I fail to understand why people say accountancy is boring,' he says. 'Numbers are marvellous. You can communicate with numbers – like annual accounts to the City. And it is exciting to find new ways of reconciling accounts, or a new way of doing a spreadsheet.'

Michael Landy is an artist who has taken the logic of work as an expression of self to the most extreme conclusion. His latest work consisted of every item he owns, including his car, broken down into constituent pieces, each meticulously labelled and then destroyed. He has been left with literally nothing, not a single possession. It is an eloquent statement about work as a means in itself rather than a means to a materialist end, and about workers – artists and accountants alike – striving to find ways to make their work unique. 'It'll examine consumerism as a way of life,' he explained beforehand, 'and ask why people increasingly invest all their dreams in it,' (The *Times*, 16 October 2000).

Of course, artists have always seen their work as an expression of themselves, and society has accepted this more readily for them than for other sorts of worker. It is easy to accept a new sculpture as a work of self-expression; harder to see a new spreadsheet in the same light. But they are essentially the same. Both are expressions of our abilities, interests and imagination.

Adding values

Our work is our calling card to the world, so we want it to reflect our values. How we work, who we work with and what we work on speaks ever-louder volumes about who we are and what we stand for.

Affiliation to political parties is weakening as classes dissolve and the dash for the centre accelerates. Meanwhile, companies have become more powerful. Who we work for has become a more important political act than who we vote for. A tick in a box for a party that differs marginally from the party in the next box is an act of trivial significance compared to the choice we make about where to invest our time, energy and brains on a daily basis.

And the more closely work is woven into our identities, the more picky we get. US tobacco companies struggle to find talented staff, despite above-market salaries, because few people want to work for companies that lie and kill.

We are voting by vocation.

When Shell got into hot water over Ken Saro-Wira in Nigeria, graduates dropped off their recruitment stream. Ethical concerns are becoming paramount in consumption decisions; similarly, work is becoming an ethical choice. Nine out of ten European workers say they are more loyal to firms that are 'genuinely committed to solving social problems,' according to Stephanie Draper.

And as work becomes an extension of our personal values, we are more likely to invest in it. One of the biggest 'problem' areas for the 'long hours culture' is in the charitable sector, where people are working long hours neither for money nor because their bosses demand it. They 'work' long hours because they are part of an environmental pressure group or an organization that helps disabled children, or campaigns against racism or provides disadvantaged young people with the skills to succeed in life.

Andrea Cahn is a regional director of Special Olympics, an international charity that runs sporting, training and events for people with learning difficulties. 'I work long hours, I suppose, and on the weekends,' she says. 'But I don't mind that. I don't see it as an intrusion. When you have a passion for something, and your work is about realizing that, you can't ever resent the time you spend on it.'

For people like Cahn, work is the realization of their own values and talents. It is part of life's mission. For people who see work as an opportunity to put their values into action, it is never 'just a job' – it is a lifelong campaign.

The greatest secret in the world

Most people who work say they need the money. Few are fortunate enough to be able to ignore paid employment for long. But in survey after survey, people also say they would keep working even if they did not need the money. And lottery winners prove the point.

Simon Fullerton-Ballantyne won £1.89 million in the lottery. He quit work and then later returned to buy the company he used to work for. He says, 'It's not money that makes me come to work. You have to have something to get up for in the morning otherwise you might as well not exist.'

Roger Robar won £5.8 million and bought the restaurant he once worked in. He cooks there three nights a week and says 'Cooking's in my blood. If I can't cook, I'm miserable … Why stop doing something that makes me happy?'

Economists, needless to say, have a label for this kind of behaviour. They attribute it to the rise of the 'post-scarcity' society. In advanced economies, the time when people were working to provide themselves with the things they need has long gone. And yet people do work, and work hard at that. If the purpose of that work was merely the acquisition of desirable consumer items – stuff we want but don't need – then lottery winners would quit at once. What is it that drives rich people to stay in their often low-paid, low-skill jobs?

Robert Wuthnow argues that in a post-scarcity society, 'the values associated with work shift increasingly toward emotional and intellectual gratification, collegiality, and service.' He quotes from a speech given to a group of fresher students by the chair of a large corporation. 'Since work we must, like breathing in and breathing out, let me share the greatest secret in the world with you. I tell you that good, first-rate work is glory.' In the course of his speech the chairman describes what he means:

'Good work separates humankind from the beasts.'

'Good human work puts us all together.'

'Good work builds.'

'Good work adds to the sum of humanity.'

'Good work pays.'

'Good work makes us matter.'

'Good work is fun.'

Wuthnow cites the speech as a prime example of the new formulation of work. 'In place of the work-for-money argument that seems to be of so little use, I want to suggest an alternative perspective: that people work in order to give a legitimate account of themselves.' Accounts are sociology-speak for stories – for the scripts we write for our lives. As Wuthnow puts it, accounts are 'a vital element of the process by which we ascribe meaning to our behaviour.'

In a world in which other forms of account, such as where you are born, which God you worship, or your family situation (place, faith and blood) have declined in importance, the 'legitimate account' work has acquired new salience. Our work is the principal character in our story of ourselves.

Marx was wrong! (and right)

The notion of work as an account of ourselves directly contradicts the most powerful critique of capitalism around, the one developed by Karl Marx. (He, incidentally, only felt really able to work once the boils on his backside got really bad.)

One of the central themes of his analysis is that workers are 'alienated' from the product of their labour – and that the capitalist is therefore able to scoop off some surplus value. Here is how he put it:

What, then, constitutes the alienation of labour? First, the fact that labour is external to the worker, i.e. it does not belong to his essential being; that in his work he does not affirm himself but denies himself; does not feel content but unhappy; does not develop his physical and mental energy but mortifies his body and ruins his mind.

But workers today say that their work *is* part of their essential being. And as the economy becomes based more clearly on knowledge and skills, the gap between producer and product is narrowed. In many cases, such as many service sector jobs, the worker *is* the product.

Marx wanted a world in which you could defy occupational classifications, and spend the day between fishing, weaving and reading without being a fisherman, weaver or scholar. He wanted work that was chosen and fulfilling. But as sociologist Eliot Freidson points out, Marx had little realistic and positive to say about work that was not 'alienated' – despite the fact that his own certainly was not. 'There is a kind of work about which Marx and most other writers have been silent,' Freidson says. 'The opposite of alienated labour. For that type of work I will use the phrase "labour of love".'

Hannah Arendt has tried to plug the Marx-shaped gap by asserting the difference between 'labour', a biological and economic necessity, and 'work', which is intrinsically human and creative. In his early writing Marx actually did something similar, dividing work into two types: the drudgery necessary to keep society ticking over, and fulfilling creative work – '*travail attractif*'. But while workers under communism would no longer be alienated, Marx resigned himself to the fact that the necessary work would never really be fulfilling. Reg Theriault has some problems with this:

The reasoning begs some questions about work. Would work, the work needed to be done in the world to keep it functioning, never be free and fulfilling (*travail attractif*)? Is work's only reward to be found in credited leisure time? Marx and Marxist scholars after him, merely danced around this question … the worker's existence vis-à-vis his job.

Capitalism has evolved in a way that has reduced the alienation of workers from their product, making work more human as well as more humane. A revolution has taken place with not a single shot fired. As management gurus Jonas Ridderstrale and Kjell Nordström put it, 'The workers do own the means of production; 1.3 kilograms of brain holds the key to all our futures.' But Marx's warning still stands: work that is not part of our 'essential being' is alienating, oppressive and exploitative. It is just that now we have the choice to walk away.

You can go your own way

Those who don't know by now that 'the career' is dead are almost certainly dead themselves. It's ridiculous – anybody would think we liked the old buffer and are sad that he's gone.

The obituaries of the career have filled millions of column inches.

Listen to this description from academic Audrey Collin of what we've lost. 'A succession of related jobs, arranged in a hierarchy of prestige, through which persons move in an ordered, predictable sequence.' If that was the career, then good riddance!

It is worth remembering that the word 'career' is derived from the word for a single, straight pathway. Now we are starting to meander off, following our own courses, seeking out new routes. We've gone walkabout.

There are those who lament the passing of the 'job for life'. What are they on? Who in their right mind sees a job for life as a *good thing*? Not the British people, over half of whom, given the choice to sign a binding job contract for a very attractive job for as long as they liked, went for three years or less. A job for life sounds like a jail sentence, especially to younger workers.

William J. Whyte's famous 'Organisation Man' is virtually extinct, thank goodness. The old-style corporations with steadily moving upwards escalators were always traps. Thirty years ago Theodore Roszak described the 'gentle tyranny' they exerted on their victims, making their lives comfortable and bland.

Alfred Olivetti saw this and made the jump. A keen athlete, he competes in triathlons and biathlons across the American South. He's good at it. It's the most important thing in his life. But with a doctorate in political science, he ended up as an academic and then civil servant. One day in 2000, he just gave it up and started a small sports shop in an unassuming concrete shopping plaza on Hilton Head island, South Carolina.

'When people see the PhD on my card, they often ask if I can do something about their foot, or whatever,' he says, laughing. 'They think it must be in sports science or physiology or something; they're blown away when I say it's political science. I spent every day in a suit and tie – now I wear casual clothes and bring my dogs to work.'

He works much longer hours now, and feels the stresses and strains of any business owner, but gets a huge kick out of it. 'This is who I am, this is what I do,' he says. 'I just love it.'

Olivetti is part of the mobile generation. Workers in their fifties say they have had four major jobs in their lives; those in their thirties have already had that many. In the US, the average 32-year-old has had nine jobs.

The new mobility disturbs some. Elizabeth Perle McKenna, in *When Work Doesn't Work Anymore*, says that the 'future of work will be characterised by … high staff turnover', a development she says 'might be considered good news, were it not for the fact that so many people today derive their core sense of identity and self-worth from the work that they do'. It does not seem to occur to Perle McKenna, and many others, that it is precisely *because* work is so central that people are searching for the right job for them. And the right job today will not necessarily be the right job tomorrow, because we all change – and our jobs, and work, have to change with us.

Moving is good. It signals a search for work which resonates with who we are. In the old world of careers, the trend was to follow a set track until middle-age and then have a 'mid-life crisis' of identity. Today's workers are smarter – they are refusing to get stuck in jobs that are wrong for them.

Academics in the careers field describe the rise of 'zig-zag' or 'boundaryless' careers in a desperate and largely futile attempt to try to make sense of the new fluidity. 'Without employers' orderly structures, external guides for action, and linear career paths, however, just what is the future of career?' asks Suellen Littleton in *The Future of Career*. 'When "the career" devolves to the level of the individual does free agency prevail and a form of "career anarchy" result? Is there anything that can be concluded about careers if everyone seems to be doing their own thing?'

Her answer is yes, but the real answer is no. It is probably time to give up on the term career altogether. Rather than following a pre-cut path we are going our own way, taking new avenues, making mistakes, learning, growing, exploring, lurching. It might be anarchic, but it's a whole lot more fun.

The career is dead; long live careering!

John Stuart Mill would have approved. In his essay *On Liberty* he said, 'He who lets the world, or his own portion of it, choose his plan of life for him, has no need of any other faculty than the ape-like one of imitation.' Attacking the Calvinist view that we should all know our place, Mill lamented the rise of a 'narrow theory of life … and the pinched and hidebound type of human character which it patronises'.

The ability – and requirement – to create our own working lives rather than having them laid out for us by corporate parent-replacements, embeds work still deeper into our lives. We have to think about work because no one is doing the thinking for us. There are fewer predictable ladders to climb.

For some people, especially those who entered one kind of workplace only to see it disappear, the shift from career to careering has been tough. It often seems easier to follow a plan passed over to us. Mill saw this a century and a half ago, in relation to the religiously ordained rules laid down before people. 'Many persons, no doubt, sincerely think that human beings thus cramped and dwarfed, are as their maker designed them to be; just as many have thought that trees are a much finer thing when clipped into pollards … than as nature made them.'

The same point is made, in inimitable style, by management guru Tom Peters. 'I don't want to go in the same door to work, Monday through Friday, for 41 years, like my Dad did. I think his work life stunk. (Sorry, Dad.)'

Nonetheless, the change has not always been easy. The shift from clearly signposted careers to richer and more turbulent working lives has altered the foundations of our security, as Andy Westwood, a researcher at the Industrial Society, points out:

Security was once based on one employer, or at least one set of skills, but now security comes from an ability to move with the times. I think some of the difficulties of the last few years have been the birth pangs of a different kind of working life, with different kinds of security.

Tim Penfold, 26, gave up a job in a large management consultancy to set up on his own. It is demanding. 'I have to invest in myself; I have to keep updating my knowledge.' But he says the rewards easily outweigh the downsides:

I like the independence and the flexibility. When I first decided to work this way, my father was quite nervous about it – he's retired but he'd worked for the same company for 35 years. He can see why I choose to control my own career path now, though. Working for the same company would drive me nuts (*Observer*, 23 July 2000).

The world in which working lives, careers, were laid out like tramlines before us, in which we had to decide which pigeon-hole to pop ourselves into, is thankfully passing away. Our work is under our control as never before. It therefore sends an even louder message to the world about who we are.

Good or bad, chosen or forced, paid or unpaid, work is what defines us as individuals and as a society. After eating and love-making, work is the most common experience of adult life. We spend the majority of our waking hours working: unsurprisingly, it powerfully shapes our psyches.

So we want work that stimulates, work that gives us room to grow, that paints a picture of the world through our eyes. The Japanese painter Hokusai used to sign his works 'Old Man Mad About Painting'. That's what we all want and need. To be mad about our work.

chapter three
learning curves

'It is a madhouse,' says Juan Arena, chief executive of Bankinter, an e-focused Spanish bank, of his workplace. 'Every time I come in here it's like injecting cocaine in my veins. People are shouting and working with passion and transmitting knowledge. I love it.'

Arena hated his original Madrid offices – 'all the dark wood panelling and heavy drapes' – so moved the firm to a modern, open-plan space that fits with the open-necked atmosphere of the company. 'It has been one of the most fascinating experiences of my professional life,' he says (*Financial Times*, 22 November 2000).

Bankinter is succeeding because it sees itself as more than a company. It sees itself as a crucible for ideas, a generator of intellectual energy. Not a workplace, a thinkplace. And it works, not just for the firm but for the individuals working there, who feel challenged, taxed and stimulated. With jobs like these who needs drugs?

We are now workers by brain, not hand. Work has become more intellectually stretching and demanding for more people. It's great news. Workers on factory lines have traditionally had to 'shut down' in order to survive. Now we all need to be switched on to survive. Humans are thinking, conscious creatures and our work is now allowing us to think, rather than requiring us to sideline the very part of us that makes us uniquely human.

Our work reflects and identifies who we are. But, critically, it also determines who we will become, what and who we know, what skills we acquire, what lessons we pass on. Work is a lifelong voyage of discovery.

Our work is the biggest adventure there is.

Helen Keller said that life is either a daring adventure or it is nothing. Our work is the biggest adventure there is.

Work engages our critical faculties. It is absorbing. It stretches our intellects and stirs our passions, unless we are in the wrong job. Terkel describes it as 'a search for astonishment'. Work is where we develop ourselves, intellectually as well as personally. The fast pace of change in the world of work, which many see as threatening, is a golden opportunity. It's true that new skills are constantly required – both technical and more importantly, personal skills – but acquiring them gives us richer choices and more interesting lives. Companies bizarrely send people on personal development courses when work itself is the ultimate, lifelong personal development course.

People used to learn and then earn. Now we learn as we earn. We want to build networks as well as pension funds. We want equity but we want excitement too. And the new labour market offers more opportunities than ever before to invest in our own personal capital through work.

Caroline Soeborg Ohlson, chief creative officer of Cell Network, the world's third-largest internet consultancy, says the new economy is allowing people like her to rewrite the work script:

We tell stories – that make a difference for our employees, for our customers, and for the world around us. A new story about life and work is simply more exciting and fulfilling than a story about the industrial way of living (*Fast Company*, September 2000).

Destination: work

When your grandchildren ask you, 'What did you do during the work revolution?' you want a good answer. Pick one of the following:

◆ 'Well, I got myself a dull, secure job that I could do without too much trouble and that didn't take too much out of me.'

◆ 'I hopped around a lot, learning all the time, and searching for work that would stretch me and use all my talents, and I found it along the way. It was hairy at times, and I often wondered what I was doing, but it was quite a ride!'

If you think (a) is the right answer, why on earth have you read as far as Chapter Three? Put this book down immediately and go and check your electric blanket. Assuming you're still here, that means you want work that engages you. And let's be honest, it's pretty unlikely you are going to find it at the first shot.

Peter Drucker, management consultant to the corporate stars, puts it in blunt terms. 'The probability that the first choice you make is the right one is roughly one in a million. If you decide that your first choice was the right one, chances are you are just plain lazy.'

Drucker is right. In the film *Keeping the Faith*, the Jewish mother of the Rabbi in love with the gentile who is loved in turn by his Catholic priest friend (oh, go and watch it) says, 'It takes at least ten years to learn enough about yourself to stop being a complete idiot.' She's talking about relationships, but the same can be said of many workers. Who really knows what path they want to follow when they come of age?

Job-hopping is about the search for work that gets our pulses racing. This casts a new light on discussions about job turnover. High levels of job-changing are typically seen in a negative light. Robert Wuthnow, one among many, laments the fact that ten million Americans change occupations each year, especially those with higher levels of skills. 'These changes [are not] limited to persons in less desirable jobs where higher turnover rates might be expected,' he says. 'They are actually higher among white-collar workers with college educations.'

In his survey, Wuthnow found that three out of four workers had been in more than one line of work (excluding jobs as students), half had been in three lines of work, and one in ten had been in five or more. Younger British workers have already had more employers than retirees. We are workers on the move.

And a good thing too. John Stuart Mill was ahead of his time on this, as on many issues. 'Human nature is not a machine to be built after a model, and set to do exactly the work prescribed for it, but a tree, which requires to grow and develop itself on all sides.'

To develop on 'all sides', most people need to move through different jobs. Job-changing is not about insecurity, it is about a search for Terkel's 'daily meaning'. It is OK for a former jazz clarinettist to move world financial markets, as Alan Greenspan, Chairman of the US Federal Reserve, now does. The fluid, self-charted nature of modern work lives is allowing more people to put their passions to work. This is a huge improvement on stuffier, static labour markets, which often pushed individual passions outside the world of paid work, giving birth to the gifted amateur.

An 'amateur' is someone who is highly skilled at something that they do without being paid, simply for the love of it. Amateur pursuits are 'work', in the true sense of the term. Indeed some of the most important work ever done has been by animated amateurs. In 1905, for example, a patent clerk published three scientific papers which changed the course not only of physics but of twentieth-century history. Of course, Albert Einstein later 'went pro', but at his creative peak no one in the scientific academy would hire him, such were his intellectual and personal eccentricities. The knowledge economy had not been born. Today, Einstein would set up on his own, creating einstein.com – or, more likely, would be snapped up by a hot new university or consultancy. Likewise, Charles Darwin was on the HMS Beagle as a gentleman's companion to the captain, not primarily as a biologist.

Amateur endeavour has laid the foundations of many aspects of modern science and literature. Our debt to amateurism needs to be acknowledged. But then we should ditch the whole notion. People's passions should not be slotted around 'work' but be the very purpose of their work.

Education, education, education

People without degrees often say they have been educated at the 'university of life'. Now, we are all being educated there, regardless of what letters we might have after or before our names. College is at best a foundation stone. Work is the most important component of our learning – the core curriculum of the university of life.

But modern life classes are not modelled after traditional colleges, with fixed geographical points and clearly defined course plans. Studying at the university of life (principal subject: work) now is like being an Open University student – highly flexible, life-long and entirely self-managed.

'There is no question,' says Marsha. 'Work is *the* place of adult learning. If you pay attention, you learn about the world, and other people – but also about yourself. There are people who just do their jobs and wash their car at the weekend. They aren't learning. They seem to have less stress in their life, it's true – but they seem to have much less happiness, too.'

Sue says that she learned more in her week of bakery training than at any other point in her life. 'It was really intense, I had to take in so much at once. I am still learning all the time. When you're the only person in the store who knows about bakery, you want to be a kind of expert.'

We want to learn not only for learning's sake, but in order to thrive. John Knell, in a paper on the rise of the 'free worker' points out that this is a highly individualized course of study. He cites research showing that 93 per cent of managers do not trust their employers to manage their career interests.

Knell argues that free workers – the new 'mercenary class' – assess possible job choices on the basis of how much brain-food they will get. They ask questions like, 'Will this job increase my chances of securing and maximizing future opportunities?' and 'Will the job enhance my intellectual capital?'

Highly skilled workers are not simply learning more; they are learning how to learn, and are learning faster. 'Know-how' is not enough, according to Linda Holbeche, from the Roffey Park Management School; 'learn-how' is at least as significant.

We are the experts on our own needs. No company can assess our skills needs the way we can. In any case, the skills we need might not be the ones they want to give us. Michael Arthur dubs self-conscious, self-managing workers 'career agents' who he says 'may be wiser about their own dispositions, their own learning, and their own long-term needs, than are their educational institutions, vocational advisors, and companies'.

This means more mobility, as we have already seen, which many career professionals regret as wasteful and inefficient. Arthur takes a different view. 'Every experience is an opportunity for learning. The wider the range of experiences, the wider the range of skills available to be acquired.'

'I've never had a plan, a kind of schedule,' says Charlene. 'My plan has only ever been to do great work, and to learn and grow from it. I never aimed for titles or certain jobs or anything. It just happened.'

Work is now a series of projects, each of which offers a new learning opportunity. People are dipping into different fields, acquiring new skills and sharing existing ones. In the knowledge economy, what workers want more than anything else, more even than money, is knowledge. In a study of the high-tech and film-making sectors in California, Suellen Littleton found that the employment transaction was not as simple as paying for sought-after skills:

People are recruited for skills that have been developed from previous projects [but] the system, at its best, consists of cycles in which the learning taken from previous projects is applied in the current project, which in turn provides new learning opportunities.

In economic terms, the advantages of work as a series of learning projects are enormous. One of the most persistent problems with market economies is insufficient sharing of knowledge and information across firms and between sectors. But mobile workers carry knowledge with them, rather than sitting possessively with their skills in one part of one company. As Knell puts it, 'they are the expert pollen of the new economy, moving quickly between jobs and assignments, transferring ideas, skills and attitudes.'

So a more rapid turnover of workers equals a more rapid diffusion of knowledge – and a more vibrant economy.

Reciprocity

The short-term nature of job contracts upsets some commentators, on the grounds of the costs to the individual – who in fact stands to gain – and the erosion of long-term, high-trust relationships that decent societies and successful economies supposedly require.

One of the loudest doomsayers is Richard Sennett, who argues in the *Corrosion of Character* that short-termism, in the form of a 'turnstile world of work', militates against the creation of trust as well as character. He says there is a current 'revolt against routine' and worries about the consequences for trust creation.

But there is a logical fallacy in the argument that trust is only possible in long-term relationships. Many wives do not trust their husbands of 30 years' standing; soldiers thrown together in combat can display high levels of trust without knowing each other's names.

The conditions under which trust is generated are ones in which the individual and mutual benefits of the relationship are clearly laid out. This is perfectly possible in short-term job situations. Indeed the short-term nature of some contracts increases the need for transparency, so that both sides know the deal. It may in fact be in longer-term relationships that the mutuality gets muddy and the chances of trust diminish.

Lauryn Hill sings about the need for reciprocity in personal relationships, if they are to survive. Similarly, careers academic Suellen Littleton uses the concept to describe the new employment deal. Effort and knowledge-sharing may be offered by the worker in exchange for new learning opportunities, financial rewards and new networks. And so long as both sides know the score, this can engender high levels of trust almost immediately. 'If the benefits are genuinely mutual,' she says, 'projects provide a basis for high commitment from both parties to the short-term employment contract.'

Al Gini refers to this as 'sequential loyalty' – the economic equivalent of serial monogamy – and argues that it can be strong while it lasts, but that it is transitory, fading as soon as the mutual benefit runs out. And Michael Arthur likens it to a series of joint ventures, in which 'both the company and each of its partners have vested interests in the acquisition of new knowledge, or intellectual capital.'

The heightened awareness of modern workers to the employment deal on offer is throwing fresh light on the employment contract. Trust does not come from two parties who have known each other for decades swapping vague promises. It comes when the quid pro quo is crystal clear.

The growing breed of 'interim managers' (IMs), parachuted into gaps in corporate structures, personify these new partnerships and the possibilities for short-term, high-trust working relationships. *Personnel Today* magazine calls them a 'special breed, committed to independence as a career choice, thriving on challenge and deriving their job satisfaction from resolving problems' (17 October 2000).

Usually with varied experience behind them, these individual rapid response units learn more with each assignment (and get a wad of cash, of course), in return for the rapid application of their skills. Very rapid: most placement companies for IMs estimate that interims have about six hours in which to make a difference.

Forget burnout: rustout is the real enemy

One of the demons stalking the modern workplace is supposed to be burnout – what happens when workers simply cannot cope with the demands being made of them. Burnout equals exhaustion, breakdown, end-of-the-rope time.

Real burnout is terrible, the work equivalent of a heart attack. But it usually happens only when someone ignores all the warning signs: feeling low, bitter, trapped, sleepless and so on. And it doesn't happen to someone who is loving their work. It happens to people who feel forced into sticking at unsatisfactory jobs.

Philosopher Michel de Montaigne said that people who don't listen to their boredom threshold when reading a book are like those who ignore their pain threshold. The same is true of jobs. Ignoring the boredom threshold is like ignoring all those chest pains – and then wondering how on earth that burnout/heart attack could have happened.

There is, in any case, a much bigger danger than burnout. People who stay in jobs which no longer stimulate or satisfy them are exposed to a much more widespread affliction, what Richard Leider, author of *The Power of Purpose*, calls the 'rustout syndrome'. Describing a senior executive trapped in a cul-de-sac, Leider captures the essence of the disease. 'He felt trapped in a kind of vocational quicksand. He was not challenged. He felt he could not leave, nor could he succeed. In short, he was rusting out.' Rustout happens to someone who is not 'challenged by meaningful tasks and is spared the positive stress surrounding such tasks.'

Marx identified a kind of rustout syndrome in his description of alienated labour, work in which the worker 'does not develop his physical and mental energy but mortifies his body and ruins his soul'.

Some jobs 'mortify' from the very beginning; the only mystery is why anybody stays in them or why society tolerates them. But even the best of jobs loses its lustre after a while. For people who thirst to learn and stretch, the feeling of becoming good at their task quickly evaporates to be replaced by a sense of boredom as soon as they can do it. As Leider says, 'the fact is that satisfaction always leads to dissatisfaction!'

The latest survey from the Chartered Institute of Personnel Directors confirms that the longer people have been in their jobs, the less likely they are to find them satisfying. Once we accept that work is part of our journey of self-exploration, a lifelong learning opportunity, we shouldn't find this either surprising or unsettling. Once the learning curve begins to level out, our interest drops too. If we stay put, we become rustout risks.

The lesson is this: if you can do it, stop doing it and go and do something more interesting instead.

People who are in jobs they can 'do with their eyes closed' have almost certainly closed their eyes.

Group genius

Most universities now offer MBA programmes. Thousands of suppliers now offer 'webucation', or e-learning. There are tens of thousands of books teaching us how to be more successful at work (the best of which, of course, are to be found in the *momentum* series). But none of these developments has in any way diminished the importance of the most powerful teaching mechanism any of us will ever encounter: another person. To be more precise, a successful, talented, inspirational, knowledgeable, intellectually generous person.

The fastest way to learn is to work alongside a gifted person. It is also the fastest way to plug into great networks. Smart workers are seeking out great teachers and shouldering their way through their corporate doors. In the new economy, we are all apprentices. So people want to work with Martha Lane Fox, rather than for lastminute.com; for Richard Branson rather than for Virgin.

It doesn't stop with finding a bionic boss, of course. We also want to work in high-performance cultures with creative co-workers. Von Stamm suggests that two of the top three priorities for skilled job-hunters are that the company is an 'intellectual meeting place' and that the people they will work with are good. This matters because we want to work in a brainy environment and because we can learn more from a few days working with ultra-smart people than from a thousand days of being 'trained' in badly-lit rooms, drinking bad coffee.

Bruce Mau is a man people want to work with and who goes out of his way to hire people *he* wants to work with. He describes his world-famous design studio, BMD, as 'an ecology' and says 'It can only absorb certain kinds of people … I feel like a guardian. Bringing in the wrong kinds of people poisons the garden,' (*Fast Company*, October 2000).

When he needed to hire people, Mau put a quiz in the newspaper. Under his favourite catchphrase – 'Avoid fields. Jump fences' – he asked 40 questions, including 'Who made a film consisting of nothing but the color blue?' (Answer: Derek Jarman.) The ad was the talk of Toronto and he lured some top-flight designers to the firm.

Mau generated suspicion at his old firm, Pentagram, for being too absorbed by his tasks. 'I was working late a lot, because I was interested in the work,' he explains, 'and this partner said "no one here works like that."'

So Mau set about creating a place where people could work like that. His manifesto for BMD includes advice such as:

Don't clean your desk. You might find something in the morning that you can't see tonight.

Ask stupid questions. Growth is fuelled by desire and innocence.

Drift. Allow yourself to wander aimlessly. Lack judgement.

Stay up late. Strange things happen when you have gone too far, have been up too long, have worked too hard and are separated from the rest of the world.

Designers would kill to work at BMD because of Mau himself, because of the brilliance of his hand-picked staff and because of the atmosphere of experimentation he creates. BMD offers what everyone wants from their work: intellectual stimulation and opportunities for learning and personal development. 'A big part of why people come here is for the adventure and the journey,' Mau says. 'It allows them to go down roads that they haven't been down before.'

Historically, genius has been seen as a lonely gift. But today most people go along with Mau's view, in theory at least, if not always in practice, that two heads are better than one. To flourish, genius needs the right conditions – in Mill's terms, it 'can only breathe freely in an atmosphere of freedom' – which means the right corporate culture.

Consultancy firm KnOwhere specializes in getting people to think more effectively together, a cerebral collaboration that they believe produces breakthrough results. People thinking together – what KnOwhere's Gail and Matt Taylor call 'massively parallel processing' – requires no hierarchy and maximum individual freedom of action. (Mill would like KnOwhere.) The quality of ideas generated is better than any individual could have managed alone. The team is greater than the sums of its parts; what the Taylors call 'group genius' is unleashed (*Fast Company*, October/November 1997).

Work is the happy pill

Despite all the improvements in work over recent decades – the increased room for growth and learning, the opportunities for self-development, the chance to work with great people, the chance to write our own work script – there is still an ingrained attitude that happiness lies outside work. That we are waiting for the weekend. Friday has a magical status in the anti-work world. We celebrate TGIF with happy hours. Chris Evans thanks 'F' it is Friday. 'It's Friday, it's five o'clock, it's *Crackerjack.*'

In the collective consciousness, work is a time of woe, while holidays are happy time. The notion that we are happier when we are not working is so deeply embedded that it is difficult to challenge. But the plain fact is this: we are happier at work. We may not think it, but it's true.

Mihaly Csikszentmihalyi has, on top of an improbable name, what in our current culture is an improbable argument – that work is the real source of happiness. In *Flow – The Psychology of Optimal Experience*, Csikszentmihalyi examines the nature of happiness. He argues persuasively that happiness involves a lack of self-consciousness, an absorption, quoting Mill: 'Ask yourself if you are happy and you cease to be so.'

The optimal experience correlated with happiness is a state in which 'people are so involved in an activity that nothing else seems to matter; the experience itself is so enjoyable that people will do it at great cost, for the sheer sake of doing it.' Csikszentmihalyi calls this state 'flow'.

Small children are often in 'flow', or 'in the moment', tongues pressed against lips as they colour or do dot-to-dot. (Some of us still do it. The tongue–lip thing, not dot-to-dot.) Athletes describe this feeling as being 'in the zone'. Flow occurs when we are engaged and absorbed, when our minds are wrapped up in the project at hand. It is not quite the same feeling as pleasure, which often comes later. Dorothy Parker, when asked if she enjoyed writing, replied, 'No, I enjoy having written.'

The theory of flow seems uncontroversial. But when Csikszentmihalyi asked people to register times when they felt in flow, he found to his surprise that work was the clear winner. Half the time people were at work they were in 'flow', compared to 18 per cent in their leisure time. Manager-level workers were in flow more often than blue-collar workers (64 per cent and 47 per cent) – but both experienced flow at work much more often than at home.

We may not literally whistle while we work any more, but a level of unselfconscious absorption is certainly in evidence. A man called Rollie, interviewed by Richard Leider, says of work that it 'must be a turn on; it must feel passionate'. A turn on, perhaps – but it also tunes everything else out, puts us in flow and makes us happy.

Csikszentmihalyi also asked people to record when they would 'rather be doing something else' during a particular period of time and found that it was more likely when they were at work. He calls this the 'work paradox':

In other words, motivation was low at work even when it provided flow, and it was high in leisure even when the quality of experience was low. Thus we have the paradoxical situation: On the job people feel skilful and challenged, and therefore feel more happy, strong, creative, and satisfied. In their free time people feel that there is generally not much to do and their skills are not being used, and therefore they tend to feel more sad, weak, dull and dissatisfied. Yet they would like to work less and spend more time in leisure.

Why is this? It is puzzling to Csikszentmihalyi, although he speculates that the problem lies in 'the modern worker's relation to his job', that because we assume we are working out of necessity rather than choice, work time is 'perceived as time subtracted from the total available for our life'.

He suggests that we need to get better at using our leisure. Maybe. But what we certainly need to do is shatter the negative psychology surrounding the activity that makes us happiest: work.

The truly fulfilling nature, the 'flow', of work has been buried under several metres of bad press about work, inspired by Calvinist Christianity, early industrialization and twentieth-century consumerism. As a result, we are in a position where work, which is more fulfilling than ever and is the primary source of our happiness, is continually portrayed as our enemy. It is no wonder that we are so screwed-up about work. Because the truth is that work is the best time of our lives.

Work is our campus, our journey to self-discovery and the foundation stone of our happiness. We are learning on the job, searching for the right job, loving the job. And when we stop loving and learning, we leave. This is the new world of work. And it works.

Katharine Graham, the president of the *Washington Post* during the Watergate scandal, said, 'To love what you do and feel that it matters; how could anything be more fun?' The only thing that could be more fun would be to do it in a great place with people that you love. And that's happening too.

chapter four
there's no place like work

Terry Wogan has never done a day's work in his life.

Terry Wogan has never done a day's work in his life. 'What I have done for nearly forty years has not been work,' he says. 'It's not a proper job. Work? Toiling down a mine, that's work. Digging up a road, that's work' (*Radio Times*, 26 August 2000).

For Wogan, an activity can only be 'work' if it meets two criteria: it is physically hard and it takes place in an unappealing environment. Because his life's work has consisted of talking – a lot! – and entertaining people in front of microphones and cameras, having lots of laughs and making lots of friends along the way, it has, by contrast, been 'a piece of cake'.

But Wogan's work is today's work. Few people now toil under arduous or hazardous conditions. Most people work in safe, clean environments. Modern workplaces are a long way from the dark satanic mills of industrializing Britain. Increasingly, work environments look, feel, sound and even smell great. Air-conditioned offices with agreeable art on the walls are no longer the exception. Indeed, for many people the work environment is physically superior to the home front.

Not that the change has happened overnight. Just as it took decades for factories to be reshaped following the introduction of electricity – for a long time, activities were still grouped around the old fossil-fuel power source – it has taken time for workplaces to abandon industrial modes of operation. For many years, offices were laid out and run like factories, with desks in rows resembling production lines, strict rules about uniforms and everyone, literally, knowing their place.

All this is changing. Until fairly recently a young woman wearing chinos and a casual blouse curled up on a sofa flicking through a paper was decidedly (a) at home and (b) at leisure. Now she's just as likely to be at work.

The services available to workers are beyond the dreams of workers just a few decades ago. One of the first campaigns waged by the Industrial Society, in the early part of the last century, was to persuade factory owners to provide toilets for their workers. (Don't dwell too long on how things must have worked before that.)

A century on, the workplace has changed beyond recognition. There are toilets of course – for women, as well as men – but there is a growing array of other services besides: showers, cafés, gyms, crèches, chill-out rooms, medical services, counselling, prayer rooms, shopping facilities, massage. The twenty-first century workplace lays on more than the average neighbourhood.

Everyone knows that we live in a service-led economy. But this has taken on a new meaning. When we are at work, we are not simply producing services, we are consuming them too. Meet the new family provider: the firm.

Where are you going to go today?

On a fine day, Trevor Bateman opens his patio doors and has a barbecue for lunch. People grab burgers and beers and sit in casual shirts on the wooden terrace, looking across the lake and chatting with friends. A typical weekend scene: except that it's a Friday, the location is the office of Electronic Arts, in Surrey, UK, and the patio doors are 20 feet high. Electronic Arts, a computer games company, works out of a Norman Foster building that is designed to be a pleasant, aesthetically pleasing place to work. Bateman, the Facilities Supervisor, says he loves his work, and his workplace.

Once united by grey functionality, workplaces are now competing to have the biggest atrium, the water feature with the most bubbling sound, the best use of light. It is all a long way from the factory floor. Job satisfaction in call centres – described by some as the 'sweatshops' of the new economy – has been shown to be enormously affected by the physical environment. Colour, light and space can transform attitudes and productivity, according to an international study by the *European Industrial Relations Review*. Thomas Cook has redesigned its centre in Falkirk so that staff walk through a 'sensorama' corridor each morning 'to be greeted by the sound of waves crashing, bright changing colours and the smell of coconut oil' (*Guardian*, 9 October 2000).

The Kajima building in Japan has a birdsong-filled atrium and a scented garden. There is some music, but it varies according to the time of day. People bring trays of food around every now and again – the Eastern equivalent of the tea trolley. Professor Derek Clements Croome says that all the senses need to be considered. 'Touch is often forgotten – we need to be surrounded by natural surfaces such as glass, wood and stone,' (*Guardian*, 27 October 2000).

Much of the multi-sensory office rhetoric sounds downright flaky, and that's before we get the Feng Shui experts in. And of course a sponge-washed wall does not compensate for a deathly dull job. Nor should it. But the fact is that we are sensory beings and an environment that soothes and pleases our senses is a huge improvement on one that goes out of its way to offend them. We want, for example, to be in natural light and near natural objects. And many modern workspaces recognize this need. Outside areas, like the Electronic Arts terrace, or internal courtyards, help to meet the need. British Airways has a huge glass-covered 'street' complete with real trees in its Waterside offices near Heathrow Airport. The Department for Education and Employment, setting an appropriate trend, has a huge central atrium with trees and a water feature.

George Michaelides, whose media company works around a single large table near windows, says, 'I don't believe anyone can work comfortably without masses of natural light. And without working comfortably you can't work efficiently.'

If there is no nature to hand, firms can grow their own. Another.com, in North London, has a real lawn in the centre of the office on which picnic-style meetings are held. 'It always reminds us not to let the grass grow beneath our feet!' says founder Graham Goodkind (*Viewpoint*, Issue 08).

Work activities are increasingly diverse: thinking time, reading time, writing time, meeting time, idea-sharing time, online time. Workplaces are adapting to meet these different needs, fitting the space to the work. Rather than just being stuck in one place – i.e. behind a desk – workers are increasingly moving to the most appropriate space for their current activity, or their personal taste.

HHCL, a marketing consultancy, contains a range of 'work zones': desks; 'huddle rooms' – glass-sided meeting rooms; a U-shaped alcove with bench seat and table, for quiet work; a café; small creative rooms; a therapy room; a bright, stand-up room for fast meetings; and Pitt Stop, a stand-up computer station for quick searches.

For those who do work mostly from one place, personalization is the key. At Electronic Arts, employees can control the lighting and temperature for their work stations from their desktop computers.

happy mondays

momentum

Xperts, a Virginia-based IT consultancy, gave staff £1,000 each to decorate their work spaces any way they wanted. Some choose Greek-style statues, some oriental rugs, others minimalist wooden surfaces. Far from undermining corporate loyalty, allowing individual expression increases people's sense of attachment. Xperts sales supervisor Kay Larkin says, 'When you are allowed to make something yours, it makes you feel more part of the company,' (*Fast Company*, September 2000).

Latte labourers

The boundaries of what constitutes the 'office' are shifting. Lots of us can work from pretty much anywhere – home, a park bench, the beach – so long as we have the right electronic gear. The automatic link between 'work' and 'place' is being eroded. Work is where you want it to be.

And while many companies have brought café culture into work, others are sending work out to the café. In the coffee shops dotting modern cities there are as many laptops as lattes. A number of City firms encourage staff to hold meetings in coffee shops off-site. Starbucks, ever-alert to a new trend, has installed boardroom tables in some City outlets.

Andrew Harrison, a partner at DEGW, a leading architecture firm and a man who thinks about space more than anyone except the most ardent Trekkie, says the use of different places for meetings – cafés, museums, parks – reflects the dispersal of the 'office' into the city.

He says the change reflects the way organizations are changing. 'There are more partnerships now, the lines between companies and organisations is less clear. The great advantage of a coffee-house is that it provides neutral ground, and project space.'

The new economy – based on networks, shifting collaborations, rapid start-ups – needs new spaces and many companies and workers are finding them on their doorsteps. Just as the line between domestic space and work space is blurring, so the line between public and corporate space is harder to see. Corporations are going cosmopolitan.

For smaller firms, which are unable to create campus-style corporate villages, access to third spaces means a central urban location. Easyshop, which sells underwear online, is based in Finchley, an outer London suburb – but has made plans to move into the centre of town so that staff can access bars and cafés for meetings, networking and socializing. As Andy Westwood says, 'The great irony facing Internet companies is that they increasingly need to be in the sorts of exciting central locations that technology was supposed to allow them to avoid.'

Of course commerce and coffee is not an entirely new blend, simply one that was lost for a couple of centuries. While café culture tends to be associated today with literary or philosophical activity, remember that Lloyds of London started in a coffee-shop. These days, work comes with a biscotti on the side. Welcome to the espresso economy.

Homework

By now we are all supposed to be working out of rose-covered thatched period properties, linked only by fibre-optic cable to the outside world. Knowledge work was to be the new cottage industry, according to forecasts made just a couple of decades ago. 'Telecommuting' was going to change the world. It hasn't happened. More people today say that they work from home, but for the vast majority of these that means one or at most two days a week. Only a tiny minority are genuine telecommuters.

So what happened? Forecasting is, of course, a dangerous occupation at the best of times. Danish humorist Storm Peterson says, 'it is difficult to predict – especially the future.' In this case, the forecasters forgot that people like to go to work. And the level of personal interaction required in the new wired economy is paradoxically greater than in the old one.

But workers are deciding that going to work should not necessarily mean sitting behind desks all day. They are popping out for a coffee or a walk. And they are demanding more comfort. People generally don't want to stay at home – work is simply too attractive – so the alternative is to bring all the home comforts to the office. Sofas and stereos are no longer startling office additions.

The new offices for Members of Parliament have fridges, dimmer-switch lighting and easy chairs that convert to small beds. Tellme.com, in California, has installed loft beds, on platforms above workstations.

And in the ultimate expression of homely work, The Fourth Room, a marketing consultancy, has fitted out its townhouse HQ in the style of, well, a townhouse, complete with sitting room, kitchen and dining room. Chief executive officer Piers Schmidt originally wanted a communal home and workplace but discarded that idea as impractical (for now). 'Finally, we thought: if we can't all work at home, why not bring the home to the office? We want to foster a more domestic environment. Our housekeeper will monitor the vibes and say, "Right, time for lunch."' Lunch is taken around the large kitchen table.

A relaxing work environment may seem like an oxymoron, but with companies relying on the quality of people's thinking, they are recognizing that their most valuable asset is the mindsets and attitudes of their workers. So they are making them feel right at home.

The entrepreneur's new clothes

In the same vein, why force people into uncomfortable clothes? The notion that going to work means putting on a standard uniform, that entry to the world of work requires adherence to a rigorously enforced dress code, is rightly being discarded.

It started with 'dress down Fridays' and has become dress down every day, or at least 'decide-what-you-want-and-need-to-wear-yourself-rather-than-having-to-look-it-up-in-the-staff-handbook day'. Ben and Jerry's, the hippy ice-cream company, instituted 'dress up Fridays', when staff would come to work in suits – just for a laugh.

The idea of work suits involving something unnaturally constricting, either a collar or a pair of tights, is a legacy of the view of work as a penance. Yes, 'work clothes' tend to be uncomfortable, but work isn't about comfort, damn it. You're not supposed to feel good.

Now that people are beginning to see work as good and as an expression of their individuality they are starting to wear their own clothes rather than a uniform. Not so very long ago, Richard Branson was seen as a bit of a maverick for not wearing a tie (Bill Gates was a techie, so that was OK). Now you sometimes struggle to see anyone wearing one. Arthur Andersen, one of Britain's big four accountancy firms, recently announced that male staff no longer need wear ties. And when Jack Welch, the CEO of General Electric, held a press conference to introduce his successor Jeffrey Immelt, both men wore open-necked button-down shirts and sports jackets.

Of course, there are some jobs, such as police officer, that are likely to keep uniforms for a while at least. But even the boys in blue are giving the uniform a dressing down. The Metropolitan Police, the

London force, has announced that Rastafarian dreadlocks can be worn by officers.

Dumping the tie is not the trivial issue it might seem: a survey by the HR consultancy William M. Mercer found that casual dress is what most attracts twenty-somethings to a firm, ahead of flexible work arrangements, which came second, and access to technology, ranked third. Jim Matthewman, a partner at the company, says job hunters see corporate attire as an indicator of corporate attitude. 'It is about management style, and approachability,' (*Personnel Today*, 10 October 2000).

The concierge

A busy person's To Do list is always full, both with work-related and domestic tasks. Typically, the latter have to be squeezed around the former, with workers rushing to the shops at lunchtime, dashing to the supermarket in the evening and fixing the car at the weekend.

But that was *so* twentieth century. Today plenty of workers can be ticking items off their domestic lists while they work. At Merck's New Jersey campus, staff can leave the car for an oil change, drop off dry-cleaning and shoe repairs, ask the travel service to book a holiday and arrange for a wrapped gift to be sent.

On the way out of the building, employees can pick up a movie and freshly-prepared evening meal. Merck – dubbed 'Mother Merck' by the *New York Times* – is not alone. Texas Instruments' concierges will fix your car. Sun Microsystems does your dry-cleaning for you.

In the UK, Accenture has a concierge service. Morgan Stanley Dean Witter and Goldman Sachs have sub-contracted 'lifestyle managers' for some of their staff. Corporate concierges will book tickets, send flowers, advise on theatre options and receive personal deliveries. 'We are there to pick up the pieces of people's busy lives,' says Jonathan Wallace, director of Entrust, a personal service company with a number of City firms on its books (*Financial Times*, 13 October, 2000).

Lehman Brothers, an investment bank, has established an internal concierge system to deal with personal requests. 'We are competing for the brightest and the best,' says Karl Dannebaum, a managing director at the firm. 'This is a way of getting and keeping them.' Companies are also trying to spare staff the hassle of the late-night supermarket stop. Microsoft and other companies are paying for a supermarket service which allows staff to order online in the morning and pick up their groceries from the chill- and freezer-rooms on their way out at the end of the day.

Like any good hotel or locale, twenty-first century firms offer a range of dining and drinking options. Many companies have introduced cafés and dining rooms. Mother Merck has private rooms which offer subsidized meals not only to employees, but to their friends and families too. PricewaterhouseCoopers, the accounting and consulting firm, lays on a bar for its thirsty knowledge workers. Other companies, such as AOL, bring the beer to employees' desks on a Friday afternoon.

Not everyone has access to these top-notch services. They are sprouting mostly in the high-tech and financial services sectors – where the hours are long and the fight for staff is fierce. But the trend is for companies everywhere to share some of the burden of modern, busy lives. It is hard, today, to imagine an Industrial-Society-style campaign for massage services for all workers. But who knows? In the meantime, every step that companies take towards realizing that people's lives do not divide neatly in two is a step in the right direction.

Blood, sweat and tears

Once the shopping's taken care of, you might feel like a haircut. No problem. MBNA bank has a hairdresser on site, and of course the House of Commons – the ultimate work-as-hotel environment – has stylists on hand for our lawmakers. How about a check-up? Netscape has a dentist on site. Companies are also offering a range of therapies. HHCL has a massage and acupuncture room.

Medical services are increasingly available in the workplace. A growing number of on-site centres offer standard medical testing and advice. Big firms in the USA offer cancer screening, blood tests and X-rays. Work, once a survival course in physically arduous conditions, has gone seriously soft, tending carefully to physical, mental and emotional needs.

Goodbye bootcamp. Hello Boots.

But it's not just about our bodies. Employee counselling is one of the fastest-growing services in the UK. Knowledge work, after all, is mind work, so companies worry as much about mental as physical health. Originally intended to help workers with work-related problems, most counselling is now general, tackling any problem which is affecting an employee's mental well-being.

Lucy, a TV researcher, went to her company's counsellor when a failed relationship knocked her sideways. 'The first time I saw the counsellor I just sat and cried,' she says. 'I dread to think what would have happened if the counselling had not been available. I think I would have left the company. I could have been on Prozac. At least half our department have been to see her,' (*The Scotsman*, 17 April 2000).

This is not New-Age, Soho stuff. Scottish Amicable, a sturdy financial institution, has a contract with the Employee Counselling Service. The director of the service, Pauline Bryan, says it pays for itself by freeing up management time that would otherwise be used dealing with the consequences of mental health problems. 'Managers [can] end up spending hours trying to help people with what are not really work-related issues.'

As long ago as the 1920s E. K. Hall of American Telephone and Telegraph said, 'We must find ways to help our workers get their worries out of their minds so they can get on the job "rarin' to go".'

A sure way to be 'rarin' to go', as well as laying the foundation of good mental and physical health, is to take regular exercise. So, no surprise, companies are in this game too, encouraging staff not only to work out their problems but work out their bodies. At 3.00 pm at Electronic Arts half a dozen staff are building up a sweat, swapping keyboards for bench presses in the gym. The firm has a running track too. Most City firms have gyms and fitness centres, or at least a deal with a nearby gym. We may work in deodorized dryness in air-conditioned offices, but it doesn't mean there's no sweat at work.

And baby comes too!

There are those who think companies have no business getting involved in people's personal lives, cooking dinner, fixing cars or clearing heads, and that Mother Merck is less helper than intruder. But one of the reasons companies are entering the domestic sphere is that the former domestic workers, women, have entered the corporate sphere.

And on top of shopping, cooking and ironing, there is one other activity which used to be left to women – childcare. Parents are not new in the workplace, of course. There have always been lots of fathers at work, with wives at home looking after the kids and nice desk photos to show they are 'family' men. But now their wives are in the next door offices, who takes care of baby? In many cases, the corporation is becoming childminder.

One in six UK firms now offer childcare facilities, an eight-fold increase on ten years ago. In the US, where women have cut deeper paths into the corporate world, nine out of ten large firms offer assistance with childcare. And in a recent survey, 75 per cent of American workers said they felt comfortable raising personal or family issues with their supervisors, up from 65 per cent a decade ago. People are taking their work personally, and taking their personal stuff to work too.

Merck's childcare centre has been a big draw for talented workers – especially, though not exclusively, women. Diane Hook, the firm's director of business and organization consulting, who has two daughters aged four and two, says the childcare centre drew her to the firm. 'Both my children are happy,' she says. 'I can't say enough about it. It's stable. It's not going to close. We [she and her husband] have total peace of mind,' (*New York Times*, 12 December 1999).

The provision of childcare services is a huge and hugely significant expansion of corporate responsibility. It gives the term 'family firm' new meaning. The advantages for parents are huge. They can pop to see their children during the day, they are with them until the moment they start work and again from the moment they finish and it makes it easier for mothers to keep breastfeeding.

The divide between work and life, between home and office, between public and private closes further. Fashionable management theorists talk about bringing the 'whole person' to work. What's happening is that people are bringing the whole family to work.

In areas where the struggle for staff is most acute, some firms are even allowing parents to bring their babies into the office itself. The Kansas Insurance Department is one of the pioneers, bringing cots into cubicles and allowing burping during brainstorming sessions. 'It just allows a parent to be a caregiver,' says commissioner Kathleen Sebelius, who made the policy change. 'Parents don't have to make a choice about "Am I a parent or am I a worker?" And people are nicer to each other if there is a baby around,' (New York Times, 4 December 2000).

Even supporters admit that most workers will be less productive when they are simultaneously caring for baby. But if the person is good enough, they'll live with that. Gay Warren Gaddis, CEO of T3, an advertising and marketing company in Texas that has introduced a Babies Welcome policy, says, 'I know they will be distracted' [the employees, not the babies]. 'Still, being here at 60 per cent is better than totally missing that person.' This is the ultimate in worker and parent power: love me, love my baby.

In the good old days, of course, granny might have been around to care for the little ones. Today she's on the other side of the country, or even the world, or maybe running her own business. Or perhaps she needs caring for too, another need being identified by Caring Corp. Four out of ten large US firms now offer eldercare referral services, twice the proportion of just ten years ago. A handful of companies in the UK are offering 'granny crèches' to provide care for elderly parents.

Companies have not suddenly discovered a long-buried conscience about the need to care for children and the elderly. If they can make it easier for people to solve care concerns, they make it easier for people to stay on the job. It takes an average of 16 hours to find a childcare or eldercare place, mostly during what would normally be working hours. For the company, a helping hand goes straight to the bottom line. But if it makes life easier, who's complaining about the motive?

Working in mysterious ways

Having fed, massaged, exercised and treated us, then taken care of our relatives, the modern corporation worries next about our souls.

The relationship between work and worship is an old one, as described in Chapter One. Historically, work has been a punishment from God or a penance paid for God. Spiritual development and business development remained entirely separate spheres. The closest most of us have got to religion at work is ending up working with an OTT evangelical Christian with a disturbing tendency to drop 'Have You Met The Lord?' leaflets in your in-box, particularly the morning after a night on the tiles.

But the relationship between work and spirituality is becoming more subtle, more complex and more significant. People are looking for work that expresses their individuality and reflects their values – and for some that includes their faith. Organized religion is losing favour, but an increasing number of people describe themselves as 'spiritual'. Work is helping to plug this gap.

Local churches are seeing the number of rears on pews drop year by year; the number of workplaces where prayer, worship or meditation is taking place is on the rise. In the same way that work has come to be a provider of comfort and services, it is replicating the local place of worship.

As Joanne Ciulla, author of *The Working Life – The Promise and Betrayal of Modern Work*, puts it, 'When churches, mosques and temples can't compete with the demands of the workplace, they move into it.'

Merck, needless to say, hosts bible study groups. Shell UK has experimented with a Buddhist priest – one of a growing band of 'corporate clergy'. A number of companies have meditation rooms. At Boeing, in California, staff can go to Torah, Koran or Bible study classes.

A Muslim worker at Boeing says 'Before I had to spend two and a half hours a day to go to the mosque and pray. Now we schedule it like any other meeting.' Again, the idea of taking religion to work is not new – Britain has a long and rich tradition of 'industrial chaplaincy' – but it has acquired new force.

Ciulla quotes the collection *Spirit at Work* by Jay Conger, which describes how the workplace community is taking on the spiritual functions of the old neighbourhood. 'The growing hunger for community offers new doorways for spirituality to enter and enrich our workplace,' he says.

Danah Zohar even argues that after IQ and EQ (emotional intelligence) comes a new set of skills for the modern world – SQ, spiritual intelligence. Given that most people see themselves as spiritual beings and that most people spend a lot of time engaged in work, it makes perfect sense to elide the two, to bring not just our bodies and minds, but also our souls, to work.

Of course, there are those who see this as another avenue for management exploitation, asking, literally, whether nothing is sacred. Ciulla is among the sceptics. 'First scientific management tried to capture the body, then human relations tried to capture the heart, and now some consultants want to tap into the soul.'

It may well be that some managers think bringing the spirit to work will bring in the cash too. They might even be right. But Ciulla is falling into the old trap of seeing the resources brought to work as a zero-sum game, as a battle between worker and management. If, instead, work is seen as the way we choose to interact with the world, contribute to the world and leave our mark on the world, then fitting it in with our faith is, if anything, a step forwards rather than a lurch back.

Of course, addressing spiritual issues at work is not for everyone, in just the same way that not everyone fancies taking communion in the parish church. Mandatory prayer meetings or pressure to conform to any kind of spiritual activity, or indeed any other social or physical activity, are bad news. It is up to us as individuals. There may be no atheists in foxholes, but there are plenty in offices.

The notion of the corporate community has been around before, in various guises. Quaker businessmen such as Joseph Rowntree and George Cadbury offered education, housing and health services. In the US, George Mortimer Pullman built a town for his employees outside Chicago and acted not just as employer but storeowner and landlord too (resulting in a strike when he dropped wages but not rents).

But while these earlier business leaders were motivated by a paternalistic, often religiously inspired, regard for the welfare of their workers, with business benefits being largely incidental, today's firms are motivated by profits.

Nobody should think for a moment that companies are offering these services out of the goodness of their hearts, out of a concern for the health of the nation. They are offering them because their increasingly demanding workers are demanding them. Because they keep staff happier, healthier and therefore more productive. It is all about the bottom line.

But just because it is good for the firm it does not mean it is bad for us. It's terrific for us. If the nature of modern work means that we, the workers, have to be treated like royalty to achieve the results the company wants, that's just marvellous. This is 'win–win' at its very best. Companies think that providing attractive places and useful services will help to keep us healthy, happy and on the job. And they're right. Work is not a miserable slog any more. It is certainly more appealing than struggling round supermarkets or ironing shirts.

Anybody who thinks work should be miserable simply because it is work or that there should be a *cordon sanitaire* between 'work' and 'life' needs to find a time machine, key in the year 1543, and go and join Calvin's crew. They'll feel more at home there. In the meantime, the rest of us will get on with enjoying our work, and our workplaces.

chapter five
social work

It used to be so simple. Sensible people were careful not to mix 'business' and 'pleasure'. Men went to work to earn the bread. Women baked it at home. The male, public world of work was focused on production, on getting things done. Idle chat was frowned upon, even if it was possible over the sound of clanging machinery.

Sure, there was some joshing over lunch or a post-work beer. But the Community – the place where men and women socialized and found friendship and fellowship – began where the workplace ended. The lines between commerce and community, between male and female worlds, were clear.

Now it seems anything goes. A growing proportion of time at work is spent talking to other people rather than 'doing' something practical. Sometimes the chat is about work, sometimes about the latest single from Macy Gray. Companies used to run 'work socials', events at which staff would mingle and play together. Now work is social. The new facilities at work – cafés, bars and sports areas – reflect the socialization of labour.

Work used to be where we would make things. Now it is where we make friends. Or even deeper connections. Work is increasingly a place where passions are ignited. Where true love is being found. Work has become friendlier, more playful and more fun – placing it more securely at the centre of our lives.

'One of the reasons work is becoming more important is that more jobs are allowing room for personal interaction,' says Michael Willmott. 'There are fewer people in mind-numbing jobs. There is a lot of concern about people in call centres – but at least they are talking to people, at least there is some engagement.' Humans are intrinsically social animals and our work is increasingly reflecting our natures.

Historian Eric Hobsbawm points out that people have always sought these opportunities. 'We know that in the country people go to the market not only to buy things but also to meet other people and exchange news and gossip … human beings don't want to be on their own, but prefer to work with others.'

Today the workplace is our everyday community. One of the reasons why telecommuting never took off the way the experts forecast is the huge value people place on the community of the workplace and the personal relationships that are formed there. As other forms of community, especially family-based and religion-based communities, diminish in importance, work takes on more significance.

'My sense is that outside of work we feel more isolated than in the past,' says Alan Halpern, who just swapped self-employment for a job with a publishing house in Dayton, Ohio. 'If I didn't belong to something at work, it'd be hard to belong to something anywhere.'

There are a number of reasons for the shift towards a more communitarian, humane worklife. First, there has been a profound change in the economics of value creation, which has encouraged, even necessitated, more personal interaction. Work is shifting away from manufacturing and towards services and, increasingly, services that need a human touch. At the same time, the trend for people to choose work reflecting their own personalities and values is concentrating people of like mind in one workplace, increasing the chances of friendship flowering. And there is a growing recognition among employers that a friendlier, looser atmosphere enhances productivity.

But there is one change that dwarfs all the others, a workers' revolution that has changed the nature of labour for good – the entry of women. The simple presence of women in the workplace has helped to create a more natural and sociable environment than the testosterone-filled offices and factories of the past. Women are creating changes at work which are deeper and more far-reaching than the most ambitious and radical change-management theorist could even dream of. Women are reclaiming work, for all of us.

Women at work

'I like to have women around … practically all the women I know feel the same way about the presence of men,' says Reg Theriault, lamenting the traditional gender division of labour. 'To be segregated from the opposite sex for the biggest and best part of the day, every day you work, is not only unnatural but unnecessary.'

Thankfully the walls of the old gender apartheid are coming down. Women will shortly be in the majority in the workplace. And while some professional separation remains, women are entering the upper echelons of management and the professions previously reserved almost entirely for men: there are now more women than men studying law and medicine.

The modern workplace is a place where men and women can meet as equals, sharing in the financial and personal rewards of work. When men worked and women stayed at home, mixed-sex socializing had to take place in non-work settings. Now the office has lost its gender, cementing its position as the new community.

Of course, women's work has resulted in constant scare stories about the impact on children, or men's jobs – and the creation of Superwoman and The Woman Who Has it All. Gender stereotyping continues – though it has changed. As Barbra Streisand puts it, 'Not so long ago we were referred to as dolls, tomatoes, chicks, babes, broads. We've graduated to being called tough cookies, foxes, bitches and witches. I guess that's progress.'

Paid work is clearly more important to women now, simply because they are engaged in it like never before. But the genderquake has made work more salient for all of us, male as well as female. When work was ghettoized by gender, the female half of the population was excluded from 'men's talk', i.e. conversations about work. Now women, with an unemployment rate half that for men, talk and care about work as much as men. 'How was your day, dear?' is now a two-way question. Work no longer divides men and women. It unites them.

Which is not to say that men and women have the same attitude to work. Far from it. Women attach much greater significance to their work and get much more out of it than men do. Let me say that again, just in case you missed it. Contrary to popular, misogynist myth, paid work is more important to women than it is to men. Paid work is more fulfilling for women than men.

Female full-time workers are more likely to say they enjoy their jobs than their male peers, and mothers rate it especially highly, according to a recent survey by Mintel. Mothers of young children who work say that they feel more valued *at home* than mothers who have chosen to stay at home.

Women are twice as likely as men to 'feel most appreciated' at work rather than home, according to Judith Doyle's survey. And women get much more out of the social side of work, with twice as many women as men saying that they enjoy socializing at work, the fun of office life and drinking after work with colleagues. 'Women seem to get more out of work,' says Amanda White, from Mintel. 'What they like most is gaining a new circle of friends,' (*Sunday Telegraph*, 12 November 2000).

The same survey revealed telling differences in the reasons men and women say they work. A third of female respondents said they worked because they liked being with other people and the same proportion said they enjoyed 'developing their career'. Half as many men mentioned these two incentives for working, with their focus on 'providing for basic needs' and 'preparing for retirement'.

The difference between the attitudes of men and women may be a remnant of the breadwinner world, when men saw work as a means to an end – a wage, which was their contribution to the family. Women are not labouring under that legacy and so are freer to express and pursue a more positive approach to work; work which is chosen, sociable and fulfilling.

Women are also demanding more flexible working patterns, more interpersonal styles of work, and more meaning from their work. Elizabeth Perle McKenna says that women 'are the most transformative and revolutionary group because we have to redefine work'.

Martine Bedin, a French designer who runs her own company, says 'I have worked above all with women, with whom I have been very close, transforming work into a feminine act, abolishing the distinction between work and life.' But the feminine revolution is making work better for men as well as women. It has kick-started the movement to make our work part of our lives, rather than an adjunct to them.

I'll be there for you

'There are young people in this very city going to work in their weekend clothes, who are doing at work what they'd as soon be doing at home for free, who are meeting their professional peers outside the office because they actually like to associate, and lingering at work because that's where they feel most comfortable. Really.' So, enviously, says Mark, the main character in Jonathan Baird's *Day Job*, a story-cum-treatise on modern work.

It is true that more of us are finding friendship at work. Of course, it has always been the case that co-workers can become comrades, but the link between friendship and work has strengthened. Seven out of ten men and nine out of ten women make lasting friendships at work, according to *Friendship Works*, a study by consultancy Sanders and Sidney. In an even more striking finding, Judith Doyle discovered that one in three of us meet 'most of our friends' through work, with women again the most likely to find work social.

Sally David from Sanders and Sidney says that firms which encourage a friendly environment reap the rewards. 'We urge companies to strengthen workplace communities and encourage friendships,' she says. 'These create a better atmosphere, improved team working and staff retention,' (*Guardian*, 12 October 2000). The increase in the number of friendships formed at work stems both from the feminization of the office – with women in the lead in socializing work – and an increase in the amount of time spent interacting with work colleagues.

There is, however, still a deep-seated attitude that sees a reliance on work for friends as somehow 'sad' or to see friendships formed at work as 'artificial' compared to the 'authentic' friendships formed elsewhere. This view of work and friendship is utterly unfounded and deeply regressive.

Why is it that making friends with someone you happen to live near, or attend the same college as, is seen as superior to making friends with someone with interests so close to your own that they choose to spend the majority of their waking hours in the same place as you, engaged in complementary activities? Aristotle said that real friendship requires a community. Today that community can be found at work.

Some argue that the 'short-term' nature of employment militates against true friendship, in the same way that Sennett and others assume that trust is on the decline. Ray Pahl, a well-respected sociologist, falls into this reactionary trap. He writes that:

employment … is more flexible and is perceived to be insecure, and the reduction of the importance of the psychological contract between employer and employee – that is, the exchange of security for loyalty – leads to a low-trust environment. As employees are encouraged to watch their own backs and be prepared to move on, they are less likely to trust and make friends with colleagues from work.

It seems, though, as if the opposite is happening. Far from shrinking from work-framed friendships, we are embracing them. Pahl misunderstands the nature of labour-market change and in particular the reason for greater mobility – or 'short-termism.' The main reason people move on to another job is because they are dissatisfied with the old one. They want jobs that make better use of their talents and which provide greater opportunities for meaningful work. And people who find what they are looking for are more likely to make friends with their co-workers because they are likely to have more in common with them than most of the other people in their lives.

Marsha has made some of her closest friends through work. As a Democratic party activist and social entrepreneur, she says that sharing values has a powerful influence at work:

What binds us together is what we believe in – that's my work, but it is also how I live my life. It is a kind of empathic knowing of each other. I am working with a group of people on a project in LA, providing health care to black communities. We go to the bar, we talk, and get engaged at an intimate level – it is not that it is separate to the work. The work is what connects us, emotionally. On the last day of the administration, for the last goodbye, at 7pm, the chief of staff stood up and said: 'Family is an overused term. But when people spend so much time together, working together, and supporting each other, that's family. And that's us.'

If we all stuck to our first choices of jobs and/or careers – striking the 'loyalty/security' deal that Pahl so fondly misses – then our co-workers would consist merely of other people who had landed up in the same rut. What makes them a richer source of friends than people who have ended up in the same place as a result of a genuine search, like Marsha's old department? Modern work – flexible, fluid and chosen – is in fact more conducive to real friendship than the career tramlines of the past. Work friendships are a cause for celebration, not commiseration.

The short-termism versus friendship argument is in any case flawed at a basic level. The thinking behind it seems to be that because the relationship between colleagues is certain to be short – with one or the other moving on at some point – the friendship will necessarily end, so there is less incentive to invest in it.

Yet people make friends at school or university, knowing for certain that the joint experience will end. This does not seem to invalidate the friendship. After all, friends keep in touch even when the circumstances – school, college, location, club membership – in which their friendship was formed change. Work is no different. Just because you move on doesn't mean that you lose touch. People keep friends from work just as they do from other walks of life.

The new strength of workplace friendship has coincided with a shift towards a 'network' economy – one in which institutions are porous to people and ideas, partnerships are the primary model for business ventures, and who you know is much more important than what you know. John Knell describes how successful workers are plugged into 'hot' networks: 'active, fast, extensive and high-quality'.

And the lines between personal and professional relationships are blurring. When people have warm relationships with business contacts and do business with friends, the separation between work and home address books is extinguished. Let's say you become

chapter five

happy mondays

momentum

friends with someone while you are working together for the same company, then one or both of you moves on. You remain friends, and occasionally put business each other's way. Then you decide to set up a new firm together. Are you friends or professional contacts? The truth is that you are both, with the emphasis shifting over time.

Ramesh says that his best friend is a former colleague, who he sees most weekends. And for him the line between worker and friend has disappeared. 'When I applied for British citizenship, I had to find two people to act as witnesses, people who had known me for more than three years. Both of them were friends from work.'

Inevitably, there are people who lament this rubbing out of the line between the personal and the professional, between private and public lives. These are the people who prefer the world to come in nicely labelled boxes: 'friend', 'colleague', 'contact', 'partner'. These are the same miserable people who say that you shouldn't 'mix business and pleasure'. Why on earth not? A life in which we divide ourselves neatly between work and cool professionalism over here, and life and real relationships over there, is no kind of life at all. Working with friends, far from being a contradiction in terms or a dangerous confusion, is one of the greatest pleasures life can bring.

Sex, love and videotape

The traditional link between sex and work, aside from those who actually work in the sex trade, has been the affair between the boss (male, middle-aged, overweight) and his secretary (female, young, slim). Given growing sensitivity to possible sexual harassment and/or abuses of power in these relationships, the slow abandonment of the sexual stereotypes underpinning them and the reduction in the number of management posts requiring a full-time personal assistant, the boss/secretary liaison is on the wane. But this has not signalled the end of sex at work. In fact, the increased sociability of working cultures and the rise in the number of women in employment have combined to turn the modern workplace into the most important mating ground in modern society. Hence the popularity of films such as *Working Girl* and *What Women Want* and TV programmes like *Ally McBeal*.

Office flings are not the exception. They are the norm. Shere Hite, in *Sex and Business*, finds that 62 per cent of women and 71 per cent of men have had a 'love affair' with a colleague. And a survey by *Globeroom* magazine finds that 64 per cent of us have had 'an affair' with a co-worker (September/October 2000). One of the fastest-growing pornography markets is in real CCTV recordings of 'office erotica'. (Tip: check for cameras first. Unless of course that's your thing.)

Mixed workplaces with lots of interaction and friendship are bound to lead to sexual relationships. Matt Thorne, in his novel *Eight Minutes Idle*, paints a fairly depressing and for most people inaccurate picture of the modern workplace. But the main character, Daniel, spends most of his time thinking about his friends at work and has a relationship with his boss, Alice – the first move being made, inevitably, in the office late at night when everyone has gone home. 'Hiding beneath a table reminds me [Daniel] of school. This is just one of the … associations that makes the call centre such a sexy place.' So there you have it.

Even call centres are sexy.

Advertisers have spotted the trend. An advert for ready-prepared food shows a man and a woman in the office, late. He asks her if she wants to join him for dinner and reads the description on the packet poking out of his bag. Eventually, she goes to leave and his face falls. But then she issues the standard nightclub line: 'Get your coat, then, you've pulled.'

The rise of e-mail communication has almost certainly increased the romantic potential of work. E-flirting is one of the most highly developed skills in the modern worker's armoury. The *Bridget Jones* diaries rightly portray e-mail as a key dramatic device in the formation of modern relationships. In one scene, she snags her man by resolutely ignoring a 'message pending' signal, knowing it to be a message from him, thus driving him wild with anticipation, the cyber-version of 'treat 'em mean, keep 'em keen'. Of course there are dangers with e-mail courting. Just before Christmas 2000, Clare Squires sent an e-mail to her lover (who was also a co-worker), complimenting him on his sexual prowess. He forwarded it to his friends and within six hours it was being read around the world.

The internet allows us to meet people 'at work' even when they work in an unrelated office miles away. One in four women polled on newwomanonline.co.uk said they had formed a 'romantic friendship' while surfing the web and now spent an average of 102 minutes during the workday, chatting online to their e-mate.

Online courting is just one instance of the way IT is blurring the line between work and life. Lots of attention has been focused on the way that laptops and mobile phones allow work to 'intrude' on 'private' time. But IT also makes it much easier to be doing something other than work when you are at work. Someone tapping away at a keyboard could be:

◆ doing the quarterly sales forecasts

◆ e-mailing a lover

- paying the phone bill
- writing a briefing for a new client
- looking for a great holiday deal

and so on. Desktop e-mail and internet access have made it easier than ever to allow life to 'intrude' on work. All of which is good news. It really doesn't matter what gets done when. If people want to flirt all afternoon and do their spreadsheet in the evening, who cares?

But the workplace is not simply a place for short-term passions. According to the Sanders and Sidney poll, a quarter of us meet our life partners through work. Judi James, author of *Sex at Work*, says up to half of us find lasting love with someone we meet through work.

The same factors fuelling friendships at work are increasing the odds of finding a soulmate. Work involves much more personal interaction than before, so employees get to know each other better.

People are choosing work that suits them – increasing the chances of finding a co-worker who suits them too.

Are these liaisons dangerous? Some companies think so, and institute strict rules for workplace relationships that almost amount to a ban (thereby simply making it more tempting, of course). Others, mostly in the USA, insist staff who form a couple sign a 'love contract', pledging that the relationship was entered into by consent and promising no sexual harassment lawsuits if it all ends in tears.

Even without formal policies on relationships, many workplace lovers feel the need to keep their relationships secret for fear that people will judge the participants differently, or question whether business decisions by one involving the other are being made objectively. This is an extension of the 'don't mix business and pleasure' adage, which is unworkable given all the changes in the world of work. As Charles Cochrane, from the Council of Civil Service Unions, says, 'Our … central office employs so many people that if you banned relationships there, I doubt if anyone would have a social life at all,' (*Guardian*, 11 October 2000).

If is also deeply reactionary to stand in the way of 'work-love'. If someone at work finds someone else at work attractive and they begin a relationship, this is good news. Good news for them, for their colleagues who share in some of the fun of a new relationship being formed, and for the firm – which is rewarded with higher productivity and loyalty if it allows the workplace community to flourish.

Of course, mixing work and love creates potential problems – but it also creates the potential for us to spend more time with the people we most want to be with, to integrate our lives and our work, and construct freer and more natural workplace communities.

The changing nature of work is allowing more people to find true love during their labouring hours. At the same time it is allowing some to combine their personal and professional passions. Particularly in sectors of the economy with high levels of business start-ups, more and more couples are becoming partners in both senses of the term.

Jo Mei Chang and Dale Skeen met at a technical conference (on database systems, if you must know) and then worked together in a new software firm, Teknekron, which was bought by Reuters in 1994. Skeen and Chang used the money from the sale to launch their own firm, Vitria Technology Inc., making infrastructure software for e-businesses. They now employ 800 people.

The line between their work and lives has truly collapsed. They host staff meetings at their house – another shared project – in the evenings and at weekends. 'Work and home are intertwined,' says Chang. 'We recognise it is inevitable, so we don't even try to stop it … when you build a start-up, the whole thing is about passion. What's better than to share your deepest passion with your spouse? We're business partners, and we are also married. I feel fortunate for that,' (*Fast Company*, December 2000). Chang and Skeen now say they cannot imagine working apart.

Even if a couple does not formally work together, they often have a shared passion which enriches their relationship. For all their ups and downs, Bill and Hillary Clinton have a joint interest in politics, along with Tony Blair and Cherie Booth, and now Gordon Brown and Sarah Macaulay, too. The subject of modern pillow talk is work.

Hot gossip

Given the outbreak of friendship, sex and love at work it is not surprising that gossip is so rife. Not that this is new, of course. Offices have always been fertile ground for rumour. 'Not surprisingly,' says Jeremy Lewis, editor of *The Vintage Book of Office Life*, 'given the amount of time we spend in these curious places, the friendships and the gossip and the intrigues and even the passions of office life may well loom larger than those of domestic life.'

As workplace friendships and passions have increased, the grounds for gossip have grown still further. According to one US study, the typical employee spends 24 days a year complaining about their boss, 21 days gossiping about and flirting with colleagues and 18 days chatting by coffee machines or in smoking rooms.

All of us crave information about important people in our lives and most of us love sharing it with others. Nine out of ten workers admit they have passed on secrets after being specifically asked not to, according to a survey by Office Angels – and eight out of ten admitted to passing the information on to at least two others 'within the same working day'. Information is power – and most of us want to look powerful.

All of which is good news for companies. Psychologist Louise Deacon says that 'gossip is the cement that holds organisations together.' So gossipy workplaces tend to be friendly ones, with effective team-working and a shared sense of direction. Coffee machines and water coolers are the standard street-corners of the office community, although gyms, bars and crèches are becoming new centres of gossip gravity.

Companies can use the grapevine, whether covertly or overtly. One manager told the *Guardian* that he regularly used gossip as a means of communication. 'If I wanted my team to work harder, I might tell a particularly big-mouthed member that someone wasn't pulling their weight … within hours everybody would become more conscientious,' (*Guardian*, 11 November 2000). By his own admission, this is 'sneaky' and is far from good management practice, but it shows the grip of the grapevine.

There are more sophisticated efforts underway to capture the value of the gossip channels. StockProject.com is designing software which turns rumour into usable fact by getting staff to anonymously invest virtual money into 'stocks' – which might represent completion dates for a certain project, annual sales or how long a particular hot-shot executive is likely to stay with the firm (*Financial Times*, 18 October 2000).

Communities of people are alive with stories, rumours and innuendo. It is part of the human condition. Workplaces, as the primary community in most people's lives, are natural homes for our instinct for acquiring and sharing information. Even people who claim to hate their jobs spend a huge amount of time – often in the pub, near work, with their work colleagues, of course – talking about who is doing what, where, when and with whom. Work is what makes tongues wag.

Playtime

Work and play are traditionally seen as opposites – 'all work and no play makes Jack a dull boy'. And advocates of play are among the most fierce critics of work. The writer Pat Kane calls for a new 'play ethic' to replace the tired work one. Putting the play ethic into action, he says, means mandatory reduction in working hours (theplayethic.com).

But the divide between work and play is artificial. It always has been – Dickens said there was no worthwhile work that did not contain an element of play – but it is especially so today. Work is more playful than ever. And smart employers know it.

In attempting to draw a clear distinction between work and play, author Jeremy Rifkin manages only to illustrate how blurred the line has become. In *The Age of Access*, he argues that the 'rules and assumptions governing play are quite different from those traditionally governing work'. Rifkin cites three attributes of play that differentiate it from work. First, 'play is enjoyable, it's fun.' Second, play is a 'voluntary' activity. Third, play is 'deeply participatory'. Leaving aside the objections to these even as true statements about play, Rifkin's views reinforce the false and regressive division between work and play.

The implications of Rifkin's view are that work is, by definition, lacking in enjoyment and fun, that people work only because they have to and that collaborative, joint efforts are restricted to non-working hours. There are a few factual problems with this view. Fact: people like their work and get more enjoyment from it than from their leisure. Fact: most people say they would work even if they did not need the money. Fact: workers spend more time interacting with each other, participating in joint endeavour, than ever before.

Rifkin is wrong, wrong and wrong again about work and play. He and others like him, by insisting on this arbitrary divide, make it harder to make work more playful for more people. Rebecca Abrams, in *The Playful Self*, argues that the inaccurate juxtaposition of work and play means that 'the ways in which work can be a source of play are overlooked … it could be argued that what makes some kinds of employment highly rewarding, and others profoundly tedious, is the degree of play in those various kinds of work.'

Fortunately, most people are getting on with injecting play into their work, blissfully unaware that they are breaking philosophical 'rules' in doing so. For work to be as fulfilling as we want and need it to be, it has to be playful. Jeremy Bentham wrote that there are two ways of doing injury to people, 'one, the introduction of pains; the other, the exclusion of pleasures. Both are acts of tyranny.' Work which is not tyrannical must not only keep us safe from pain; it must also bring us pleasure.

More and more firms have games rooms, sports pitches, social events and cultures designed to encourage play at work. British Airways hired Paul Birch as a 'corporate jester', paying him to persuade managers to chase each other with water pistols. US comic-turned-consultant Claire Berger says the aim is to 'banish boredom from the boardroom and dullness from the desk'.

Some of the antics of the new 'humour consultants' are not for all of us (allowing staff to dress up their boss for the day springs to mind), but the deeper point that play, fun and humour all make work better is incontrovertible. Laughter is known to be good for mental and physical health, so keeping straight-faced at work is a Benthamite tyranny. Similarly, happy workers are more productive workers and most people are happier having fun.

Play can't be bolted on to an intrinsically stiff workplace, nor mandated by management, as a number of firms have found to their cost. Electronic Arts has a football pitch and initially the human resource staff tried to organize an inter-departmental league. It failed and was abandoned. Immediately, the pitch filled up with people just messing about, then gradually organizing themselves into teams of their own choosing until finally someone started a league table. The goal (no pun intended) is to create the right climate, lay on the right facilities and then just let nature run its course. The fastest way to deflate people is to send them on courses in fun.

When work is playful, it is even harder to see the disappearing line between work and life. Abrams describes two women, mothers of five children between them, who run a flower shop in Oxford. Twice a week they get up at 4.00 am to drive to London for supplies. By Thursday evening they are 'exhausted'. Just before Christmas, Victoria and Sue – who work 'long, hard hours' – hung hoops of ivy and scarlet chilli peppers on their wall in place of traditional holly. 'You two are just playing!' Abrams said to them, on seeing the display. 'Yes,' they agreed happily. 'We are!'

Play is a commercial asset in other creative industries too. Marketing consultancy Play, based in Virginia, lives up to its name, helping clients such as American Express, Calvin Klein, PricewaterhouseCoopers and Disney with their campaigns. Co-founder Andy Stefanovich says that playing with ideas is the way to create killer solutions to client challenges:

That's what playing is all about. It's an attitude and approach that encourages boundless thoughts. It helps you let go of parameters. If you think about it, you were at your most creative as a child, because you had no fear. You took more risks. No one judged your performance and said you were 'bad' at playing. Our process tries to recapture some of that freedom (*Fast Company*, January/February 2000).

All the Play staffers pick their own job titles. Stefanovich's dog has its own business card (job description 'top dog') while he is 'in charge of what's next'; there is also Buzz, Whatif, Houston We've got a problem, #17, Voice of Reason and 1.21 Jigawatts. The company lives out the description by Michael Toms and Justine Willis Toms, authors of *True Work*, that 'one of the best opportunities about work is that we get to invent games that allow us to play together.'

Staff at Play are friends too. 'Play is my life,' says John Morgan. 'And I don't mean that in a cheesy way. But this is definitely not just a job. When I go home, I'm no different than when I'm at work. The clothes that I wear to band practice are the same clothes that I wear to work. My friends on the weekends are my friends at work. They come to hear my band play … We have a passion at Play that is deeper than anything I've come in contact with.'

Play suffuses our work. Fun is on the corporate agenda.

It's Monday, it's 9.00 am: it's playtime.

chapter six
are we being absorbed?

Work is at the centre of modern life. It has taken on an unprecedented individual, family and social significance. From dry-cleaning to diaper-changing, from sex to stress counselling, from picnics to prayer meetings, work is the new community.

Campaigners for a better 'work/life balance' are swimming against this tide. The distinction between the two is being eroded physically, socially and emotionally. As psychotherapist Suzie Orbach puts it, 'For most people, work is where life is now.'

Work is pulling more strongly upon us. Work is how we identify ourselves. It is what stimulates us to learn and grow. It is where we spend time in agreeable surroundings with colleagues, friends and lovers. For some, these are troubling trends. The salience of work is seen as dangerous, a collective equivalent of Mrs Thatcher's famous lack of a 'hinterland' – a life beyond work. Companies, in US academic Arlie Hochschild's phrase, are 'absorbing' us. An invasion of the life-snatchers is underway.

If work becomes too important, the worriers contend 'Won't that be bad for individuals, families and communities,'? 'Shouldn't we be fighting the encroachment of work?' Well, no. The fears are misplaced and based on an outdated, downbeat view of work.

There are four principal concerns voiced about the growing space occupied by work in our lives:

◆ that the social ties that bind society together are becoming weaker

◆ that individuals are investing too much of themselves in an inherently risky proposition

◆ that workers are being conned into giving up too much of their time to work

◆ that home and family life are suffering from the competing
attractions of the modern workplace.

happy mondays

momentum

Rending the social fabric?

The first charge is that work is destroying 'real' i.e. geographically based communities. Social commentators and politicians are spending a lot of time right now fretting about the apparent fraying of community ties. Anglo-Saxon economies are supposed to be running down their stocks of what Harvard professor Robert Putnam calls 'social capital' – the networks and institutions that bind society together. Putnam, Amitai Etzioni – the man who coined the word 'communitarianism' – and others worry about PTAs struggling to find members, churches with falling rolls, community groups running out of people with the time to help them out. But community ties are not loosening. They've just moved into the workplace.

Work has become the central crucible of social relations. Putnam *et al* worry that people don't even know who their neighbours are. But who cares? All neighbours have in common is a postcode. People certainly know who their co-workers are, and they have plenty more in common with them. There is a neighbourhood nostalgia underpinning much of the concern about community that blinds social analysts to the new forms of community being constructed under their noses. They also worry about community responsibility – but workers are the primary force behind companies having to act more responsibly.

Community is not dead. The neighbourhood is not dead. Civic spirit is not dead. Friendship is not dead. Romance is not dead. They are all alive and well – in the workplace.

What matters is that society is built on strong social connections and communities. It doesn't matter whether those communities are based around a shared location, a place of worship or a place of work. In any case, the people who are actively building workplace communities don't necessarily turn away from other communities. There is evidence that people who are active in the workplace are likely to be active in other spheres too. In the USA working mothers are much more likely to join a school PTA than their stay-at-home peers. Companies increasingly provide employees with opportunities to contribute to the broader community, for example, through sponsorship of local schools or partnerships with charities. Social capital generated at work can spill over into other communities.

There is no evidence that people are less community-minded, less concerned for the welfare of others, or less sociable than before. We are simply using different tools in different places to express our civic leanings. Work is a hugely important site for community-building, and becoming more so.

All eggs in one basket?

Work has become pleasant. It's now a place where we can play, socialize and mate. Increasingly, work meets our needs for identification, stimulation, a social life, community and even spiritual development.

This is all very well, some argue, until the P45 drops into your in-tray. Then it's not just a question of losing a job, it's a matter of losing a life. David Strum, in the *Financial Times*, describes the benefits available in the modern workplace as having the 'lasting value of a piece of chocolate cake'.

It's clear that leaving a job, whether by choice or not, is a much bigger deal when it provides more than just a pay-cheque. 'For many of us the relationships at work tend to take on more emotional meaning than the ones at home,' says William Pollack, a psychologist. 'So if something bad happens at work, it's like your spouse has divorced you or your mother or father have abandoned you.'

Losing a job damages mental health more than splitting up with a partner, according to research by Andrew Oswald at the University of Warwick. This is not a shocking finding – although plenty of people were shocked by it. For a start, there are plenty of people with jobs they like more than their partners. And the better work gets, the more likely this is. But even today the loss of a job clearly means much more than the loss of a pay-cheque. It's about the loss of the wellspring of our very identity, our place in the community, our imprint on the world.

Ilene Philipson describes the impact of being out of work on a group of women in California:

… there is work that is life, connection, recognition, and identity. There is betrayal. And there is the void, the sense of amputation from not only the specific job, but from human community and one's sense of place in that community.

Is it wise, then, to invest so much of ourselves in work? Joanne Ciulla thinks not. Her argument is strong: she accepts that work has, for many people, become more attractive and more fulfilling. But she highlights the danger of banking so much on work, just at the point in economic history when it has become so insecure:

Of all the institutions in society, why would we let one of the most precarious ones supply our social, spiritual and psychological needs? … It doesn't make sense to put such a large portion of our lives into the unsteady hands of employers … The problem is, to what community of prayer will the Boeing employee turn when he is downsized?

Ciulla asks that 'in an environment where employment is precarious' people remain connected to 'activities and organisations outside of work'. She warns us not to put all our eggs in the rickety work basket.

There's is no denying that the pain of losing a job is enormously greater if that job has been a gateway to a community, fun, friendship and fulfilment. Does this mean we should insulate ourselves from this pain, by investing less in our work? No it doesn't.

Again, there's a parallel with personal relationships. If you build a life around a partner, invest your hopes and dreams in them, make build a community of friends with them and make a home with them, then losing them will be more painful than if they were just someone to watch *Frasier* with. The more you love somebody, the more exposed you are to the pain of losing them. It is tempting, then, not to love someone too much, not to invest too much of yourself in them in case they bunk off and leave you. But this is no way to live – rationing your feelings as an act of self-preservation.

Similarly, it's true that if you put your heart and soul into your workplace community you make yourself more vulnerable to its loss. And you can't be 100 per cent certain that you won't be fired. But what is 100 per cent secure? Life involves risk and the fuller the life lived the bigger the risks taken. A world of certainties would be a very dull one. As fourteenth-century Japanese writer Kenko said, 'the most precious thing in life is its uncertainty.'

Hochschild says of her study of workers at a *Fortune 500* company that she calls Amerco:

Life at work can be insecure; the company can fire workers. But workers aren't so secure at home either. Many employees have been working for Amerco for 20 years but are on their second or third marriages or relationships (*New York Times*, 20 April 1997).

Of course, we are free to take a low-risk approach to work if we want. We can do our jobs efficiently, collect our salaries and be polite to co-workers, but pass on the session in the pub. We can choose to keep our work in a box and devote our emotional energy to other people and other pursuits. The level of investment is our choice.

But many of us choose to take the risk. We spend most of our waking hours at work and with our co-workers. We have a choice about where and how we work. And most of us would rather find work and workplaces that we want to invest in, that we want to get more out of than just a monthly pay-cheque. Yes, there are risks. But the rewards are great too.

And even if the axe does fall, the amputation is rarely absolute. True, the ex-employee is no longer formally part of the community at their former workplace – but in most cases, some friends are kept after departure. Relationships do not end simply because one party has left the building.

Ciulla, like many others, overstates the riskiness of the modern labour market. Of course there is a risk of redundancy, but the idea that we're all working under a dangling sword of downsizing hugely over-dramatizes the actual situation. Most job changes are voluntary, not forced. Average job tenure in the UK has not changed in the last 20 years. Young people, it's true, are moving jobs more frequently than their parents did – but most of this is self-generated search activity, not the result of rapid-fire redundancies. And maybe, just maybe, people who love their work and put their hearts into it are actually less vulnerable than those who are in it just for the money, just as the people who risk their hearts are more likely to make their relationships work?

People are highly adaptable. In just the same way that when we move cities we are able to put down new roots, form new relationships and find new services and networks in a new neighbourhood, so we can up sticks and go to a different work community if necessary.

If work is where the heart is, of course work can break our hearts. But work is not unique. Anything or anybody that we invest heavily in has the power to hurt us. We grieve the loss of anything or anybody that has been precious to us. Because life is uncertain, the only way to avoid pain is to be careful to hold nothing dear. But who wants that?

Lulled into long hours?

The third charge levelled against work is that it is hoovering up our hours. One in four British men works more than 48 hours a week, a higher proportion than anywhere else in Europe. Four out of five executives breach the 40-hour mark. One in nine employees is working more than 60 hours a week and four out of five workplaces retain staff who are working more than their contracted hours. US workers have just overtaken their Japanese counterparts to be the marathon runners of the working world, clocking up almost 2,000 hours a year on the job. You've heard all this stuff.

Hence the current rhetoric about work/life balance. 'The long hours culture is alive and well,' said employment minister Margaret Hodge, unveiling the *Work-Life Balance 2000* survey. 'And it is making us ill.' (Ms Hodge then says that she herself works 'ridiculously long hours', of which more in Chapter Seven.) Work is supposed to be sucking too much out of us. Companies, cunning organizations that they are, are tricking us into working longer hours by laying on all the new services described in Chapters Four and Five.

The story goes something like this. Your company offers a new perk, say, a gym, a dry-cleaning service or a free manicure at your desk. The chances are you're thrilled. But beware. Your employer has joined a new and sinister group – The Absorbers. These firms introduce schemes to make your life easier, on just one condition: that you hand it over to them. That you work 18-hour days and at weekends; that you eat, exercise, play, even sleep in the office in the service of their profits. Given low unemployment, firms can no longer rely on the threat of joblessness to keep your nose to the grindstone. Without fear, they are turning to favour.

There's no doubt that a more pleasant environment, a wide range of services, friendly co-workers and interesting activities can make work a pretty attractive place to hang out. As one city lawyer puts it, 'Given the choice between sitting at home waiting for the gas repair man and staying in the office and letting the concierge service do it, there's no doubt in my mind that I'd choose the latter.'

Conclusive proof! People prefer to spend time at an interesting job than doing something mundane at home. Work is 'guilty as charged'. Except that people are making these choices for themselves, and they are pretty smart. They are not enslaving themselves to companies in exchange for a shop-to-office supermarket service. It may be that people are able to work longer hours because some of the other demands on their time have been lessened, or because they have friends at work. But this is a valid, positive choice.

'We are now seeing a reversal of the "leisure class" phenomenon,' says Jonathan Gershuny, the UK's number one expert on time use:

Once leisure signified high status, but no longer, now the most important people are the busiest, so, runs the argument, we demonstrate our status by our lack of leisure. Higher-status jobs are also the most demanding, and interesting – often these jobs are pretty much identical in content to what the leisure class used to do *as* their leisure … might we then not choose to work hard at them, and for relatively long hours, precisely because they provide an alternative source of the sorts of intrinsic benefits that might otherwise come from leisure activities?

Yes, we might. And we are. When work was bad, long hours were bad. When work is good, long hours are good news. They mean people are doing what they want. Take this simple test yourself. If you had the choice between (a) working an extra hour and picking up your clean clothes on the way out, or (b) going home to do your own laundry for an hour, which would you pick? If you picked (b), there are a couple of possibilities. Either you have a strange attraction to dirty clothes, or you are in the wrong job.

The allegation that people are being forced to work long hours is, as the next chapter shows, one that is difficult to make stick. The people working the longest hours are, by and large, in parts of the labour market where the demand for skills is very high. In other words,

happy mondays

moment um

they have enormous power over their employers. They can dictate the terms of their employment. They could, if they chose, demand to work shorter hours. Companies in desperate need of their talents would have no choice but to acquiesce. But by and large the demand is for an environment and services that allow them to keep working. Why? Simple. Because they like their jobs. Rather than worrying about working hours, we should be celebrating the fact that people are free to engage in the activity that gives them pleasure and satisfaction.

No home fires burning?

This is all very well, but what about home life? Now that women have joined men in the workplace, many worry that people – parents, in particular – are not investing enough time and energy at home. Relationships are under strain and children are suffering. Arlie Hochschild, in *The Time Bind*, describes how the growing attractiveness of work is luring people away from the home front. Tracking working families over three years, she made a surprising discovery about the motive behind the long hours worked at Amerco:

I did not anticipate the conclusion I found myself coming to: namely, that work has become a form of 'home' and home has become 'work'. The worlds of home and work have not begun to blur, as the conventional wisdom goes, but to reverse places. We are used to thinking that home is where most people feel the most appreciated, the most truly 'themselves' the most secure, the most relaxed. We are used to thinking that work is where most people feel like 'just a number' or 'a cog in a machine'. It is where they have to be 'on', have to 'act', where they are least secure and most harried. But new management techniques so pervasive in corporate life have helped transform the workplace into a more appreciative, personal sort of social world. Meanwhile, at home the divorce rate has risen, and the emotional demands have become more baffling and complex.

It is clear that people are more likely to stay at work longer if they are surrounded by pleasant colleagues and are engaged in interesting tasks in an agreeable environment. A BA executive, describing the Waterside site, says, 'The environment here does make it easier for you to stay later than you would have done otherwise.' Joe Petko, who is a regular user of the running track and gym at Merck, sometimes stays until 11.00 pm, after taking a break during the day for a run and a workout. He knows the score. 'The more they can keep you here, the more you can work.' Piers Schmidt, of marketing consultancy Fourth Room, says, 'It's not our intention, but should the office become so attractive that you never want to leave … fine.'

As jobs become more interesting, domestic tasks seem more boring. Charlene, who at the age of 32 is a senior executive handling major clients and managing over a dozen people, says:

I put all the personal stuff on the backburner. It's so tedious. I can sit at home on a Saturday morning and do nothing, while at work I get a hundred things done before lunch. The thing is, I don't want to go home and file or do tax returns! And I hate cleaning. Absolutely hate it.

Why should someone who is a knowledge worker at work want to be an administrative assistant or domestic cleaner at home?

So while the workplace is growing in attractiveness, for many people home, or 'life', is looking a bit gloomy. For dual-earner couples with children, life outside work is one of fixed timetables (childcare), conflict (whose turn is it to leave early to pick up the kids?), low-skill work (cooking, cleaning, nappy disposal) and thankless masters and mistresses (the kids). As work enters the post-industrial era, home life has become industrial.

Hochschild quotes Linda, an Amerco worker and mother of two, who personifies the issue. 'I usually come to work early, just to get away from the house. When I arrive, people are there … we sit, we talk, we joke … There's laughing, joking, fun … The more I get out of the house the better I feel. It's a terrible thing to say, but that's the way I feel.'

In Linda's case, an old-fashioned division of labour at home adds to the disparity of experience. Her husband, Bill, will do childcare when she's at work but no housework and nothing at all once Linda is home. He goes fishing at the weekends. 'He does nothing,' she says. Hochschild says that work has always provided respite from the domestic front for men, but that women have cottoned on. 'Women are discovering a great male secret – that work can be an escape from the pressures of home.'

In fact, as Linda's case demonstrates, the pull of work may be much stronger for women, because they are still expected to do the bulk of the work at home, to work a 'double shift'. A poll by *Management Today* found that 'more than 40 per cent of women admit that there are times when they see work as a welcome escape from home, whereas only 33 per cent of men said they felt the same. In the case of working mothers, that number soars to nearly 63 per cent, compared with 38 per cent of fathers.'

Judith Doyle's survey finds that the perception of home as a place of work is highest for those with responsibility for children under 13. This may explain why women rate work more highly than men. As Hochschild says, 'Women can have fame and fortune, office affairs, silicon injections, and dazzling designer clothes. But the one thing they can't have, apparently, is a man who shares the work at home.'

The work–home switch is one which women are making with most enthusiasm. Given the current division of labour, who can blame them? Why should women be the only ones to keep the home fires burning? There are some challenges for the future of families posed by the work–home switch, but these are mostly about the way working time is constructed (the subject of the next chapter).

Joanne Ciulla agrees that men have always used work as a refuge, and that 'it's not surprising that women would also use work as an escape, especially when they feel they are not appreciated at home.' But she admits not everyone is an escapee. 'Some are seduced by their career ambitions, others simply enjoy their job or their friends at work. Next to work, home life is boring for some people.'

No purpose is served by preserving the nostalgic view that while home is a loving, romantic oasis, work is a nasty, brutish necessity. It's time to recognize that for many people, the opposite is true. Or simply that even people with good home lives may be equally attracted to their work.

Novelist Gish Jen took some time off writing, worried about the toll it was taking on her private life:

I gardened, I lunched, I talked to leafleteers. I contributed to causes. I chatted with dog owners. I enjoyed my children – in the lingo of our time, I savoured them. I modelled for them fearlessness before live crabs. I modelled openness to new sports.

Jen is honest about the results of her time out. 'I found life without work strangely lifeless … I felt as if I had lost one of my senses … But most of all, I missed the orientation that came with experiencing myself as distinctly, exhilaratingly, uncomfortably, singular,' (*New York Times*, 4 December 2000).

It may be that people are choosing to invest less time and energy at home than others think they 'should'. But it's a clear and valid choice for people to be making. If they get more out of their work than they do out of their home, why on earth not?

Some commentators – though not Hochschild, who is much too sensible – pin the blame for this on work. This is a difficult case to make. Work is essentially being blamed for being too much fun, for being too stimulating and sociable. If only we could make work more miserable, the thinking goes, people would have less incentive to stay there and so would be forced to attend to their less-than-attractive home lives. But what a grisly analysis this is – that the only way to make people spend more time with people they supposedly love and adore is to make the alternatives sufficiently unappealing.

The truth is that people who love their partners and/or children and have equal, healthy and satisfying relationships with them will want to spend time with them, regardless of competing attractions. Indeed, coming home from a job brimming with stories, enthusiasm and ideas to share with a partner – and being ready to hear theirs – is a hugely positive force in relationships.

Charlene says that her work impacts on her life. 'If I'm not happy at work, that's when I'm not fun to be with. My husband and I know that we are each responsible for our own happiness, and so we support each other to do whatever it is that will make us happy. Working hard at my job makes me happier – which makes life at home better, too.'

You often hear people complain about feeling as if they 'never have enough time', that they are constantly 'torn' between their work and their families. 'I always feel as if I'm not doing justice to either,' is a common refrain.

These are portrayed as problems. In fact they are signs of huge privilege. To have a life so full that you wish you had more hours in which to live it; to have both a job you love and a partner you love, so that you want more of both of them; to be committed enough to two or more activities to want to 'do them justice' – these are not a modern malaise, as so often portrayed, they are labels of a life that is extraordinarily blessed.

We may well 'work' hard if we are engaged in an activity we love, but if we share the benefits with our families, if we allow the love of our work to spill over into the other loves of our lives then everyone benefits. Enticing work is not an enemy of personal relationships – it is a gift to them. This applies to children too. To have parents who are pursuing their passions in life is better than parents who are unfulfilled or resentful in their jobs, no matter how early they get home.

Of course not everyone has relationships like this. Some people don't want to be in a relationship at all. They are perfectly happy with their work and their friends (who may be at work). There is nothing wrong with that: it is certainly better to devote yourself to a fulfilling job than to an unfulfilling boyfriend.

And if someone is in a bad relationship, one that has no chance of competing with the attractions of work, and they choose to escape through work, so be it. There is good evidence that long hours are the result of poor personal relationships, rather than the other way around. In 'The Work Alibi – When It's Harder to Go Home', in the *Harvard Business Review*, Fernando Bartolomé finds that people in ailing relationships blamed work for their emotional problems, when there was no actual evidence of this. It is simply easier for both parties to point fingers at jobs than at their partners, or even themselves, when their relationship sours. We've all seen it. We've watched the guy who stays in the office late, doing nothing much, while his wife and young kids wait for him at home, and placed bets on the divorce date. (OK, maybe the last one is just me.)

People are not stupid, and they are not making stupid choices. If that means choosing to work at a job they love rather than going back to a partner they hate, OK. There are plenty of other, less positive ways people choose to escape – affairs and alcohol being just two. Blaming work is like blaming the presence of a lifeboat for the fact that a ship is sinking. Of course, if people are choosing to escape we might wonder if their relationships are past their sell-by dates. But that is a decision for them.

Work is getting better. It is consequently a more serious competitor for our time and energy. That's good news, given the centrality of work in our lives. It might mean that we prefer our work to other, less satisfying, activities. Fine. It might mean that we waste less time in washed-up relationships. Great. It might mean that we – especially women – demand higher standards from our partners. Fantastic. It might expose the unappealing nature of other forms of work, especially domestic labour. About time, too.

Work is not chipping away at cosy communities. It is not tricking us into giving up too much of ourselves. It is not tempting us to take irresponsible risks. And it is not hollowing out home life.

It may be that the new appeal of work is throwing an unforgiving spotlight on other parts of our lives, the ones which are supposed to so fulfilling. It may be exposing the myth of the friendly neighbourhood and life-enhancing nuclear family. It may be reducing the appeal of the local badminton club. This is all to the good. If we were only engaged in these activities for want of something better to do – and work has now become that something better – then perhaps they weren't all they were cracked up to be in the first place.

The real issue is choice. We are not being forced or tricked into work. We like it. No one who would rather be at home is sticking at a gruelling, thankless job because they have been offered a massage. People are just not that dumb. Work is good. But attitudes towards work are changing more slowly than work itself. Work is better than ever, but still the moans and groans about it continue. We still discuss work in negative, downbeat terms. We continue to bite a hand that is ever more plentifully feeding us.

Maureen Freely, a journalist and author, describes a moment when she realized how she was aping the work-is-awful rhetoric:

When I was going to work, I would say to my children, 'Oh, I know, it's awful, I wish I didn't have to go, but I have to, I'm so sorry.' But then I thought about what I was doing. The truth is that I really love my work; and that's why I was going. I was sending them the message that work was something dreadful, that you are forced into it, and I don't want them to grow up thinking that. And I was telling them that I was prepared to leave them to go and do something I hated – which is a horrible message, if you think about it. So I started telling them the truth. That I loved my work, and was proud of it.

We need to take a collective decision to do exactly what Freely did, to stop automatically attacking work and start celebrating it instead. We need to kill stone-dead the self-fulfilling prophecy that work is a necessary evil.

And then we can expect more of work in return. Once we start openly giving work our hearts and souls, we can increase our list of reciprocal demands. First up, one of our most precious commodities, taken from us during the birth of capitalism and still residing in the corporate lock-box: control over our time. We want it back.

07

chapter seven
time sovereignty

We are attracted to our work. We want it. But not in a kinky, dominatrix, kind of way. We are not slaves to our love. As workers we are willing, more than ever, to put our hearts and souls into our tasks. But in exchange we want to control the clock. We want our time back, the time which was stolen from us a couple of centuries ago.

This is not the next round of the long and largely successful campaign to reduce the length of the working week. That fight presumed that time at work was inevitably time spent dancing to someone else's tune and so attempted to increase the number of hours *we* had control over, i.e. those left over when the workday finished.

We want much, much more than this now. We do not simply want to increase the number of 'non-work' hours available – indeed lots of us like those hours less than the work ones anyway.

We want control over *all* our hours. We want to smash the work clock forever.

We want back the pre-industrial freedom to work when and where we want, in accordance with our needs and desires, rather than being stuffed into the corporate time-corset of the nine-to-five day. We've served our industrial time. Now we demand to be masters of Kipling's unforgiving minute.

What do we want? Time sovereignty! When do we want it? Now!

In search of lost time

The nine-to-five concept is so deeply embedded in popular language and culture that it's easy to forget what a recent invention it is. Before the industrial revolution, work was largely home-based and highly fluid. People worked when they needed to or felt like it and fitted their tasks around other activities – play, family, food. Joanne Ciulla points out that in the seventeenth century, working-class families rarely sat down to eat at regular times. They ate when they were hungry.

While Sunday was the official day of rest, most workers found that Monday was often needed too, declaring it, mock-religiously, 'St Monday' (arguably the patron saint of some office workers even today). Here's a description of English working habits in 1681:

When the framework knitters or makers of silk stockings had a great price for their work, they have been observed seldom to go to work on Mondays or Tuesdays but to spend most of their time at the alehouse or nine-pins … The weavers 'tis common with them to be drunk on Monday, have a headache on Tuesday, and their tools out of order on a Wednesday (quoted in Ciulla).

Before the rise of the factory, work varied according to the season, the time of the week, the weather, the mood and sobriety of the individual. Ciulla describes it well. 'Life in pre-industrial days was a bit like the life of a college student – irregular eating and sleeping, intermingled with intense drinking sessions, partying and all-night work sessions.'

This is not to suggest that people didn't work hard before the industrial era. They had to work hard to survive. But their work rates could vary day by day, week by week, or season by season. It was the task that was the measure of work, not the time. A weaver with a big order to fill might work a few 14-hour days at a stretch, then cut right back for a few more once it had been filled. Some got up at dawn and got the work done, others rose late and worked late. No one cared – so long as the job was done.

Industrialization changed all that. First, people had to leave 'home' and go to 'work' – the split which Adam Smith saw as the most important of all modern divisions of labour. Second, industrialists needed to take control of workers' time. Factories cannot work on the basis of people working when they feel like it. The industrial production process required workers to be physically present at predictable times and any 'slacking' was quickly spotted (cars missing a front right-hand window do show up). Industrialization of time sprang from the need to control production, and therefore the units of production – workers.

As Ciulla puts it, 'work required co-operation, but modern work also requires synchronization.' Actually, 'modern' work does not require synchronization – industrial work did. We are simply continuing, blindly, to ape the patterns of industrial working life long after the need for them has passed.

Industrial time was a radical departure from the natural rhythms of pre-industrial time, as the historian E. P. Thompson, in a classic essay on time and work, identified. 'Mature industrial societies are marked by time-thrift and a clear demarcation between "work" and "life". Time is now currency: it is not passed but spent.'

As such, time had to be measured more exactly. Industrialization launched the career of the minute, which though invented by the Babylonians had been largely ignored ever since. Jay Griffiths, a writer on time, quotes Thomas Hardy, in *Tess of the D'Urbevilles*, describing a pre-industrial street 'not made for hasty progress; a street laid out for … when one-handed clocks sufficiently sub-divided the day'.

Industrial work needed clocks with at least two hands. Fordist time – which reached its peak with the Taylorist 'time-and-motion' studies of the early part of the twentieth century – was exact. Factory time is bounded, punctuated by fixed breaks and measured. Workers 'clock' on and off using a time-clock, which Reg Theriault describes as 'an infernal machine if there ever was one'.

Of course, industrialists had to battle long and hard to fit workers into the schedules required by the conveyor belts of the new world and constantly complained that workers were failing to adjust. But eventually they won. Today, the industrial conception of time is so ingrained that other cultures, with a notion of time closer to the pre-industrial one, often infuriate watch-wielding Westerners.

But what Rastafarians still call 'clock time' became a social good. In Lyons, France, citizens petitioned for a town clock in the hope of leading 'more orderly lives' and so to be 'happy and contented'. Once people were clamouring for a clock, the game was up. And so, in the 1770s, a new word was born – to describe a characteristic that had never before needed a label. That word was 'punctuality'.

Clocked off

Having lost the battle against industrial time, workers had no choice but to fight for a new objective. If employers were going to control a fixed chunk of every day and every week then the goal had to be to make that chunk as small as possible, to have the maximum amount of 'free time' outside the factory gates. The fact that much of the work in factories was dangerous, unsatisfying and poorly rewarded added to the incentive to keep it to a minimum.

The tightly controlled nature of work while on the job was eventually accepted by most workers – but they wanted something in return, as Ciulla argues. 'They [workers] may have demanded a reduced but regular workday as compensation for the loss of autonomy than they suffered at work.' And so the fight over the length of the industrial day was begun.

Time was the primary battleground between workers and employers. It was seen by many as the enemy of the people. In 1894, an anarchist tried to blow up the Greenwich Observatory. And, of course, time is at the heart of Karl Marx's critique of the industrial system of exploitation – with capitalists attempting to extract as much labour value, or time, from the worker as possible. (Not that Marx's followers always got the point, though – Stalin tried to cancel the weekend.)

The long-standing tussle over time is echoed in today's debates about the need for a better 'work/life balance' (precisely what workers fought for 150 years ago) and a constant stream of scare stories about working hours. Survey after survey suggests that we are losing some of the time which our ancestors fought so hard to win for us. The previous chapter described the way in which work is blamed for the 'hurry sickness' of modern society. Silicon Valley has bred 'sleep camels', who store up sleep at the weekends then work long hours all week. 'Like dumb oxen, we work longer hours than anybody else,' laments *Guardian* columnist Polly Toynbee.

But the current debate about working hours is stuck in a time-warp. Toynbee and others are fighting the industrial battles of the past, when poorly paid workers were forced to work long hours in terrible conditions at jobs they hated. Work is not like that anymore. And the reasons people work long hours are utterly different too.

Time lords

Twenty-first century worries about working time seem, at first sight, to be a continuation of the battle for control over time between heartless capitalists and exploited workers. But they're not. The people putting in the hours– the overtimers – are not the poor huddled masses. They are senior; they are well-paid; they like their jobs; they are choosing to work the hours they do; and they have a high degree of control over their hours. Researchers at the London-based New Policy Institute, which researches social trends, considered adding long working hours to their excellent index of 'social exclusion' – until they realized that they were inversely correlated with every other indicator they measured, and wisely left it out.

While the factory time-fight was about the hours workers, largely men, were obliged by contract to work, today it is *unpaid* overtime that is ratcheting up the working-week. And it is women who are filling the swelling ranks of the overtimers. One in three mums now works more than 40 hours a week, up from fewer than one in five just ten years ago. And, crucially, the proportion of working mothers putting in unpaid overtime has soared, from 18 per cent to 47 per cent in the same period.

'Hours worked beyond the contracted hours, and mostly unpaid, are the real reason for the increase in working hours,' says University of Sussex academic Susan Harkness. 'It is professionals who are adding the unpaid hours on, especially professional women, who are catching up with the men.'

One of the most important social shifts of the last couple of decades has been the inversion of the relationship between social class and working hours. In the 1890s, the poorest 10 per cent of men were working two hours a day more than the richest; by the 1990s, the richest 10 per cent were working longer hours than the poorest.

'Bankers hours' used to mean 10.00 am–4.00 pm, with a decent lunch. Now the City boys and girls are at their desks by 7.00 am. More than 40 per cent managers and administrators work more than 48 hours a week, compared to a national average of 30 per cent. The so-called 'time crunch' is felt most acutely in households with two full-time professionals and children. This is why work/life balance is an obsession of the middle class. Al Gini says the dual-earner family 'can best be characterized as an experiment in controlled chaos'.

Why on earth are skilled workers doing so much work? Why do so many of us, on contracts that specify a 40-hour week, toil for so many more, for no additional financial gain? A popular theory is that job insecurity is gluing us to our seats – but there is little evidence for this. Just 1 per cent of those working over 48 hours a week say they are afraid of losing their jobs. Arlie Hochschild, in her work at Amerco, found no evidence that people's hours were related to job insecurity.

Two-thirds of the overtimers say they put in the hours because they are committed to their jobs. Because we are stuck in an industrial mindset that assumes work is dangerous, exploitative drudgery, we overlook the possibility that people might actually like their jobs – and may therefore put more into them. But that is what is really happening. Among those working more than 60 hours a week, 70 per cent say they 'enjoy their job', compared to 57 per cent across the whole working population (*New Statesman*, 31 July 2000).

The number of workers who say their job is 'just a means of earning a living' varies dramatically according to hours worked, from 42 per cent among those working 35–39 hours to 22 per cent of those putting in 60+ hours a week.

The long-hours workers are not afraid and they are not exploited. They love what they do.

The overtimers differ from other workers in one other regard too, the most critical one of all. They are the ones with most control over their hours of work. They have no one looking over their shoulders exept themselves. In the UK, two-thirds of those putting in over 60 hours have a say in any changes to working patterns in their organization, compared to half of those working a standard week. In the USA, half of those working over 50 hours a week say they have a flexible work schedule, compared to one in four of those working a standard 40-hour week (*Economic Policy Institute*, 21 September 2000). And younger workers are demanding more flexibility in their work schedules – the under-35s are more than twice as likely as their older colleagues to work at home some of the time.

Being a priest gives David almost total time sovereignty. 'I am obliged to conduct one service on a Sunday and attend four Diocesan meetings a year.' He says:

Otherwise I completely control my time. I think I do about 60–70 hours a week, although it is difficult to know exactly. I met some Swedish clergy who said they were not allowed, by law, to work more than 40 hours a week. I can't imagine that. Can you say to someone 'I'm sorry you've just lost your child, but my time's up now?' There is always more to do than the time to do it: and if you feel responsible you are liable to do more, rather than less.

Richard Halkett gave up a promising job with a bank, not because of the money or the work or the colleagues but because its clock had stopped on industrial time: 'I couldn't get my head around having to achieve things in the nine-to-five time frame when I'd been used to writing essays when I felt like it,' (*Guardian*, 8 November 2000). He left and now runs a dot.com, on his own time. The new economy meets the old, old economy's fluid notion of working time.

Halkett and others putting in longer but flexible hours are pioneers of an old way of working. They see a much weaker divide between work and life. They like their jobs enough to want to fit them into their lives rather than allowing them to tear holes in their lives. They are re-asserting control over their working hours. They are reclaiming time. They are demanding, and beginning to be granted, time sovereignty. And this is just the beginning.

Time sovereignty: right here, right now

The struggle now is not for reduced, fixed working hours; it is for control over our hours. The pioneers have won a degree of time sovereignty, while others, the 'time subjects', remain utterly stuck in an industrial time-zone. The ability to dictate hours is the real divide in the workplace now, not the number of hours worked. The committed leader of a charity who puts in 60 hours a week, when and where and how she chooses, is not of concern. She can leave to collect her children from school, then work on a paper in the evening if she wants.

Nor should we worry about the executive who works all weekend but can order his PA to clear his diary on Monday and go shopping. If they love their work, and dictate their own hours, who cares if they put in 50, 60 or even 70 hours a week? They deserve not our sympathy, concern – or indeed admonition – but our envy. Lucky them for having found work that they want to devote so much of their time to.

We are now in a position where the outdated rhetoric about 'work/life balance' has made people who adore their work, who see it as inseparable from their lives, who decide their own hours and who invest a lot of time in their mission, feel apologetic and guilty. Why did Margaret Hodge, the employment minister, feel the need to flagellate herself for working 'ridiculously long hours'?

Why couldn't she say 'I suppose I do work long hours, in a sense. But I don't really see it as work. I have spent most of my adult life campaigning for a fairer Britain, so to be a minister in a Labour Government is not a job – it is part of my life's work. I choose to invest a good deal of my time and energy in an activity that absorbs me and which is part of my legacy to the world. Is that a problem?'

She couldn't say this because public debate about working hours is a record stuck in an industrial groove. There are people deriving enormous pleasure from an activity we label 'work' who are having to keep quiet about it for fear of being sent to a 'work/life balance' workshop.

Certain workers are winning a degree of time sovereignty, and we all want it. Two-thirds of British workers say they would prefer to choose their own hours. Only one in five workers say they prefer a fixed nine-to-five shift; half of us say we want to work flexibly between 7.30 am and 7.30 pm; the rest of us want to be able to work whenever we choose. But while some are winning more time sovereignty, there is still a mountain to climb. Abandoning the habits of at least two centuries will not be easy. In legal and consulting firms, many contracts are still calculated on the basis of 'hours billed' – Taylor meets tort. This is nonsense. What clients want is a certain job done, not a chunk of time.

And in a radical reversion to the treatment of staff as factory fodder, a British local government office in Tower Hamlets, East London, recently decided to limit smoking breaks to two 15-minute slots a day – and force smokers to make up the half-hour at the close of business.

Leaving aside human rights and equal treatment, this case is a telling example of the way work is still constructed in industrial terms. Tower Hamlets is trying to control staff time down to the minute, an impossible task, especially for office-based work. It is perfectly possible for someone to spend 15 minutes sitting at a desk engaged in an activity other than work. Indeed, most of us find it impossible and inhumane to go through a day without some daydreaming, joking or flirting time. Some people have been known to spend more than 15 minutes getting a cup of coffee. Some spend an awfully long time in the toilet. These differences, too, must surely be accounted for in the nineteenth-century world of Tower Hamlets Borough Council.

And who is going to measure 'productive' versus 'non-productive' time? Frederick Taylor, come on down,. Tower Hamlets needs you! Bring your army of short-haired, anally-retentive young men with their stopwatches and clipboards. Or perhaps electrodes could be fitted to the heads of staff and some way could be found of measuring what they are thinking about? Then any non-work thinking time could be totted up and 'owed' to the Orwellian council.

What Tower Hamlets is saying is that somebody who works intensively for a couple of hours and slips out for a fag every now and then, and is hitting work targets, is somehow slacking, compared to someone who remains at a desk working slowly, perhaps staring out of the window or e-mailing friends. Tower Hamlets is in a time warp.

So while some small steps are being taken towards time sovereignty, industrial time still weighs heavily on the workplace. In many workplaces, people are permitted, or even encouraged, to work outside 'normal hours' (whatever *that* means now) but are still expected to work those 'normal hours' as well. Work in the post-industrial economy does not fit the standard workday well, especially given the increasing need to work across time zones. Erica takes a New York–London conference call late at night. This is OK, but she shouldn't be expected to clock on again at 9.00 am the next morning. Post-industrial working time is being tacked on top of industrial working time, when it should be succeeding it.

Time sovereignty is not about extending the nine-to-five. It is about ditching it.

Just do it

It's time to give up on time, at least as a measure of work. It's time to draw up job contracts that simply describe the job, not the hours. It's time for time sovereignty. This means: judging work by task, not time; the death of presenteeism; and allowing life to intrude on work as much as the other way around.

Using time to measure work is, as we have seen, an industrial notion. For work which was based on people performing certain repeated activities on a production line, time was a passable yardstick for work effort. But it is now well past its sell-by date. Knowledge work is not as linear as manual work. It is erratic, inconsistent and highly individual. It is taking our work back towards a more fluid, pre-industrial pattern – with bursts of demand and productivity followed by more fallow, reflective chunks of time. Knowledge work is always unbounded.

Was Archimedes bathing during his 'normal working hours'?

Thinking time is impossible to corral into set hours. Trying to make us do knowledge work within a set day is like trying to squeeze toothpaste back into the tube. Ciulla rightly says that applying yesterday's timekeeping to today's work creates discomfort: 'Perhaps what is most unsatisfying about modern work is that people frequently are paid not for what they produce, but for their time … maybe task orientation is more natural than time orientation.'

Information technology makes it much easier to drop the industrial model. Laptops, the internet and mobile phones mean that people can work when and where they want to. The common fear about IT is that it will simply tether people to the office more securely, that it will effectively keep us on the factory floor all the time. Ciulla warns that IT 'potentially makes us twenty-four-hours-a-day, 365-days-a-year employees'.

Well, yes, it does. But it makes us potentially twenty-four-hours-a-day, 365-days-a-year *non*-employees too. It allows us to work as we wish. Perhaps at a steady pace, perhaps in very intense bursts followed by long walks in the park. Perhaps between nine and five, perhaps between midnight and five, or perhaps between 6.12 am and 9.37 am, 11.05 am and 1.24 pm, 2.05 and 2.17 pm, and 4.15 pm and 7.58 pm. The point is, it doesn't matter. Ira Gershwin once joked, 'I've got a whole day's work ahead of me. I'm going to change the ribbon on my typewriter.' Well, perhaps that was one day's work – but the next day he might have written most of *Porgy and Bess*.

Time sovereignty dismisses the standard workday. It also demolishes workplace cultures that make people feel as though they are expected to be around at certain times. This disease has been dubbed 'presenteeism' or the need for 'face time'. It is just as corrosive of time sovereignty as the time-clock, if not more so. At least fixed workdays give permission to go home once the hours are done. An ever-present boss with a quip, or a glance at a watch, or a sigh, or a guilt-trip never gives that permission. Cultures can trap people just as effectively as the old factory shifts of the past, and are just as invidious and inhumane.

Of course the pressure to stick around is not new. Napoleon used to leave a bust in a lighted window so that his generals thought he was still working. And Robert Kennedy, investigating union-mob ties in the USA in 1957 (in particular the role of the Teamsters union boss Jimmy Hoffa) was heading home one night when he saw lights still on in the Teamsters HQ. Bobby ordered the car to turn around and went back to work. Hoffa, learning of this, ordered the lights to be left on every night. The exhausted Kennedy didn't get his man. (Not until 1964, anyway.)

All workers know the tricks of the presenteeism trade: an extra jacket to leave on the chair when you've gone to the pub; deactivating a screen saver so it looks like you are always at your computer; leaving visible signs of your presence early in the morning and then disappearing around the corner for a fry-up; hiding your coat and bag somewhere when you walk in late and then picking up a file to study as you saunter to your desk in shirt-sleeves looking like you've been there for hours.

But measuring tasks rather than time exposes these games as reflections of an infantile working culture. The point about time sovereignty is not to make the permission to leave ambiguous, it's to make it constant: you are 'free to go' any time. This is where time sovereignty differs from current notions of 'flexibility', which assume a normal working day that staff have to negotiate departures from. Real sovereignty means not just the legal, or negotiated, right to leave in time to pick up the children from school and catch up with work later, but the right to leave the office at 3.00 pm with no explanation at all. A culture in which flexibility has to be negotiated, or is merely 'tolerated', is not a time-sovereign one.

Time sovereignty takes the last brick away from the wall between 'work' and 'life'. It used to be possible to tell when you were at 'work' by looking at the clock. In a time-sovereign world you can be at work any time, and so not at work any time, too. Time sovereignty means it's OK to start writing a report at 8.00 pm if the mood takes you. It means it's OK to decide on a pedicure at 10.00 am if the mood takes you. You might go to your place of work and spend most of the time there engaged in non-work activities, then go home to work. The bottom line is this: to the extent that work and life are separable, it is OK for work to intrude on life – and it is OK for life to intrude on work. Take this book and read it at your desk. Later, if it's a slow day, go shopping for a couple of hours. Play tennis. Have a massage.

The facilities laid on by many firms – cafés, gyms, chill-out rooms, acupuncture – encourage this fluidity. Some corporate intranets are offering staff holiday deals, via the company's travel agents. Exult, the human resources company that runs HR for BP and others, is looking at ways of allowing financial services companies to offer home loans and so on to staff at their desks. But shouldn't they be working? Not according to Exult's head of global client relationships, Alan Little. 'If staff can work from home at the weekend on company laptops, then surely they should be allowed to book their holidays from the office on a weekday. They should be judged by results,' (*The Economist*, 18 November 2000).

Stupid firms are doing the opposite, rushing around blocking access to internet sites, monitoring e-mail and devising new policies designed to make people use their PCs for work rather than play. (Many of these firms, though, expect staff to pick up e-mails in the evening.) This is not time sovereignty, it is an attempt to prop up industrial time – an attempt which is doomed to failure.

Mr Little is a time sovereignty evangelical. He is one of a small but growing band of executives who are throwing off the shackles of industrial time. Accenture is experimenting with 'outcome-based' management. But for a true revolutionary, look no further than Sue Maguire, founder of Ideas Unlimited, a thriving management consultancy. The company is casual and playful. Maguire says she wants people to have fun at work.

But she has also created a truly time-sovereign company. 'I wanted to create an environment for people where there is no start and finish time,' she tells *Globeroom* magazine. 'There are no restrictions on holidays. If you want to take a day off work, or two weeks, take it. Let's be adult people. We have a lot of freedom here but also a lot of responsibility' (*Globeroom*, September/October 2000).

One of her employees, Karen Lynn, explains the rhythm of work at Ideas Unlimited. 'We work very long hours in periods and then we have long periods off.' Sound familiar? This is how we used to work before we were turned into cogs in the industrial machine. Before the historical aberration of factory time.

Ultimately, time-sovereign working should spell the death of holidays and even of the weekend. To many this may sound horrific, because these are the pieces of time left to us after our work is done. But it was only because 'work time' handcuffed us so tightly that we fought for this 'free time'. True liberation comes from tossing the handcuffs away altogether, from reclaiming control over our own time – not just the bits left over from work. All of it.

New times

Time sovereignty, in this pure form, cannot apply to all workers and all jobs. Clearly, knowledge work can be time sovereign. But some manufacturing jobs and front-line service sector jobs still need people to be in place A at time B. But most workers could have more sovereignty over their time than they do right now. The accountant in the car factory does not have to work 8.30 am to 4.30 pm just because the people on the shop-floor do. The marketing manager of the coffee chain does not have to work 9.00 am to 5.00 pm just because that's when the coffee is served.

People who work shifts can be given more choice over which ones to work, and more autonomy within their shifts. Time sovereignty is a spectrum; the challenge is to get as many workers as far along the spectrum towards true time sovereignty as possible.

Dutton Engineering, which makes steel enclosures for electronic circuits has abandoned a set working day or even working week and introduced a 1,770-hour working year. Staff put in longer hours to fill a big order – but then take more time off at slacker times. Sovereignty is not restricted to white-collar work.

It's not easy, though, to reform existing workplace practices. In particular, time sovereignty requires a much higher level of management skill. It's the easiest thing in the world to manage people who are physically present in a particular place between certain fixed hours. But this is not managing people's work, simply where they are parking their bottoms. It is about as challenging as taking the register of a primary school class. But it is what many know. Sociologist Jon Johnson warns that virtual workplaces will be challenging for some managers, as they will 'no longer have arbitrary control, and that means so much to organisation men'.

Many managers, 'organisation men', fool themselves that when people are looking at their computer screens they are working, when the chances are they are e-mailing their mates, looking for better deals on their holiday flights or paying their phone bills. They are allowing life to intrude on work, in the way Alan Little rightly says they should. But it is difficult for many managers to let go of the need to see their staff. As Marcia Bromit Knopf says, 'Flexible work arrangements are a kind of "letting go" model. It's saying "Here's our vision; at the end of the process we want to achieve the following goal." That way you aren't judged if you are there from Monday to Friday or from seven to seven. You are judged by what you produce.'

Managers schooled in industrial time can find this difficult. They walk into an empty office and ask the same question as the one in the BA ads of a few years back: 'WHERE IS EVERYBODY?' But if managers can't drop the industrial mindset, it probably means they're past their sell-by dates too.

Time management is bad management.

The truth is that different people work better at different times of day and under different circumstances. It is a biological fact that some people are ferociously productive early in the morning, while others are barely civil until noon and then come alive in the early evening. We can all see these different types in our homes and our offices. There are some people you know not to talk to until after 11.00 am and their second cup of coffee; others who are best avoided between 3.00 pm and 4.00 pm, when they should probably be taking a nap. Rather than trying to force individual biological clocks into an artificial workday, we should let people work when they will be most productive. For in work, as in much else, timing is everything.

There's plenty more in it for companies. Firms offering time-sovereign working will attract higher-calibre staff from whom they will extract higher value. And time-sovereign working will counter the emerging backlash against 'family-friendly' kinds of flexibility. Workers without children are starting to chafe at the opportunities for flexibility offered to those with families. Elinor Burkett, in *The Baby Boon: How Family-Friendly America Cheats the Childless*, asks, 'Why should I have to work extra hours because you have had to rush out of the office to collect a sick child?'

In a time-sovereign workplace, she doesn't have to. Parents have to hit the same targets – they might simply have to work later in the evening, when the kids are asleep. And the childless or childfree worker can come and go as they please, too. Time sovereignty means that you can walk out at 3.00 pm to collect your kids. It means you can walk out at 3.00 pm to go kayaking. It means you can walk out at 3.00 pm to go for a kip.

Many of those who support flexible working believe that it will allow us to work fewer hours. For some that may be true. But time sovereignty does not equal less work. Indeed, the evidence is that the people with the most time sovereignty are the ones who choose to work the most hours. Ultimately, the point of time sovereignty is to stop counting hours altogether. It is getting increasingly difficult to measure which time counts as 'work' anyway. Plenty of the hours spent in the 'workplace' are devoted to pleasure while knowledge work can be done on the bus in the morning or on the beach at the weekend. IT has shattered the wall between work and life, in both directions. It will soon be time to give up the attempt to keep the separation. In the end, time sovereignty is about abandoning the idea of working time altogether.

We are in the process of throwing off the shackles of industrial time, which artificially segments our lives, and returning to a pre-industrial method of working. After two centuries of time control the twenty-first century will be when we get our time back. But time sovereignty is just the first of the demands that we are making of work in exchange for our emotional and personal investment. There is a long list, a New Work Charter, in Chapter Nine.

The battle for time sovereignty can only be won if there is a successful movement to change the way works place in our lives is perceived. Work has to be reconfigured in our collective imagination as an intrinsic, central part of our lives rather than an annoying adjunct to them. Work has to be recognized as a defining feature of our humanity, rather than a dilution of our 'true selves'. Work has to be seen, potentially, as one of the loves of our lives.

Governments, trade unions, senior management, educational establishments and the media all have critical roles to play. But the chances of progress are zero unless individual workers also step up to the plate, seeking and demanding work that inspires them, holding their jobs to a much stricter account than they have done so far.

As a French tax inspector tells Theodore Zeldin, 'a job is like a love affair: if you do not love it you should leave it.' As far as your employment is concerned, you can't compromise – you have to be a lover or a leaver. But how do you know which you are? And, in either case, what do you do about it?

chapter eight
works for me

Imagine someone discussing their life partner like this: 'Well, it's just a marriage, isn't it? It'll do. I mean, there are more important things in life aren't there? I get the odd shag and I've got someone to go to the flicks with. It's OK. I mean, who lies on their deathbed saying "I wish I'd spent more time with my spouse?"'

Nobody describes their primary relationship this way. (Or at least, I fervently hope not.) Yet it's socially acceptable, even encouraged, to talk about work in these terms – despite the fact that most of us spend more time at work than we do with our partners. It's bizarre that we hold the activity which takes up most of our waking hours in such low esteem.

Consider the amount of time spent agonizing over personal relationships. Is he the right one for me? How do I know if she's the one to wed? Is it time to commit? Is this as good as it gets? Magazines – for men now as well as women – are stuffed full of relationship advice and 'commitment tests'. We fret about our compatibility. Astrologists make a fortune from telling us whether Leo and Scorpio are made for true love. (No, apparently.) The search for the ideal partner and perfect relationship is unceasing.

But plenty of the people who trawl the 'Advice' shelves of bookshops for help with finding 'true love' give scarcely a second thought to their work. They fall into jobs or careers almost by accident and then simply make do. Work is not typically subjected to the same level of critical scrutiny as relationships. All too often, we judge jobs on the basis of one or two criteria. How much does it pay? What's the commute like?

This is all wrong. We spend more hours with our jobs than with our partners. And whether we always admit it or not, our work is at least as important to our happiness. We expect relationships with people to be fulfilling. It's about time we starting treating work the same way. If your job is empty, leave. Refuse to settle for second-best. Stop adding your energies to an activity that is giving you nothing in return. Stop colluding in the 'just a job' collective sado-masochism that permits bad work to continue. Expect. Demand. Search.

In just the same way that you mull over your relationships, question whether you are in the right job. Is it giving you what you need? Does it satisfy your ambitions? Is it time to seek out a new occupation? When is it time to stay, and try to make it work, and when is it time to go?

What has your job done for you lately?

There are strong parallels between work and personal relationships: we take time to seek out people we are compatible with; there is social pressure to stick with an early choice, even if it proves to be the wrong one; following your own path often requires huge leaps of faith; and being 'lucky' in love and in work have an equally important impact on how we feel about ourselves and our lives.

Quite the catch …

It's easy to be dazzled by good looks and a wallet full of gold credit cards. Who isn't? But plastic and prettiness only go so far. They don't equal a love-match. Similarly, it's easy to be seduced by jobs or careers that deliver what society would traditionally consider to be the 'right' goods – especially money and status. Now there's nothing wrong with wanting a good-looking, well-heeled partner. And there's nothing wrong with wanting money and status. But they are not sufficient.

Joseph O'Neill is director of HIV / AIDS care and treatment for the US Department of Health and Human Services. At the age of 35 he was an up-and-coming doctor, with all the right medical schools and references on his CV. He was about to take up a prestigious post at Johns Hopkins Hospital, the pinnacle of American medicine, but he decided against it. Instead he took a job with a little-known community AIDS clinic in Baltimore. His career, eventually leading him to government, has twisted and turned many times. O'Neill draws a specific parallel between his personal journey, specifically in terms of his sexuality, and his work. The decision to turn down the job at Hopkins was a critical one. 'I remember consciously thinking, what's the point of being gay if you then just follow the straight – pun intended! – path,' he says. 'If I have resolved to follow my heart in my personal life, to find a life that fits with who I am, then shouldn't I do the same with my work?'

It can take courage to follow your heart in your work, just as it can in your personal life. Sometimes it can mean passing up apparently golden 'career opportunities', just as it can mean turning down an offer of marriage from that 'great catch'. Sometimes it is tempting to compromise for the sake of stability, to settle for less. Don't. Settle, if ever, only for more.

This is not to say that how much your work pays is not important. Indeed, if you find work that ignites your passion, the chances are you'll be paid well for it. It's just that the money shouldn't be the benchmark for the job. In the USA, workers describe their salaries as being how much 'they make' – an indication of how work has come to be seen as a mechanism for the accumulation of personal capital. Consumerism fuels the work-equals-money mantra by constantly ratcheting up the number of items, or the size of house, we 'need' in order to live well.

Consumption is not what makes us work. We want to work. But it can hold us in jobs that are meaningless to us, because of what it enables us to buy on the way home. Consumption is to a job what children are to marriage: a reason to stay, when you should really leave. And as Barbara Ehrenreich argues in *Fear of Falling*, consumption can be compensation, too, for compromises made. 'The would-be regional planner turned corporate lawyer, the would-be social worker turned banker, must compensate for abandoned dreams with spending.'

We all want nice stuff. And there is nothing, repeat, nothing, wrong with that. But nice stuff cannot and will not compensate for spending most of our waking hours engaged in an activity that we hate. Barry Schwarz warns that we can fall prey to 'thing addiction' and end up being consumed by consumption (*The American Prospect*, 11 September 2000). The work ethic was overtaken by the consumer ethic. Now it is time for the 'me ethic'.

To have and to hold?

Let's assume you are in a job. Are you going to stay in it for good? Once upon a time the 'correct' answer may have been yes. Attitudes towards careers used to mirror closely traditional views of marriage. This was a lifelong commitment. Richard Leider compares the old approach to careers to being 'train passengers who don't know where the train is now or where it's going. Often we're surprised at where it travels and where it stops, but we stay on for the ride.' Society has become more tolerant of divorce and of a diverse range of sexual lifestyles. The same freedoms need to be applied to working lives. You aren't – or at least shouldn't be – staying with jobs 'for better or worse' or 'in sickness or in health' – and *definitely* not 'for richer or for poorer'.

Younger workers are waiting before making long-term commitments either to specific employers or defined occupational paths, just as they are waiting before making the same kinds of decisions about relationships. This is good news. 'Date' lots of jobs rather plumping early for one. Guard your independence fiercely. Professor Cary Cooper says 'If you are frightened of commitment for positive reasons, because you like freedom and independence, then why commit?' (*Guardian*, 30 September 2000).

Al Gini's description of the new 'sequential loyalty' makes the appropriate comparison with human relationships. 'It is based on a quid pro quo relationship: unlike unrequited love, it must be offered and received before it can be returned, and it persists only as long as it proves mutually beneficial.' Of course this means we have to keep providing the goods. There are no free rides. But who wants to coast along in a relationship – work or personal – that is just ticking over? If it's not working, look for the exit sign.

Diss satisfaction

It is easy to know what to do if a job is making you consistently miserable, much harder if it is neither great, nor terrible – but just satisfactory. Work which is 'satisfactory' is more dangerous, in this sense, than horrible work. It can reduce the incentive to search for truly meaningful work. We can end up swapping a calling for comfort. When the devil you know isn't too bad, it may indeed seem better. The character Mark, in Jonathan Baird's *Day Job*, describes how we can be lulled into lifeless work:

No one's saying life in CS [his firm] is unacceptable. A damn sight far from ideal, but not unacceptable. It's just that the agreeability of this job, I've decided, may also be its greatest hidden danger. I make a liveable wage, I can afford to rent a decent apartment … I'm comfortable enough to put off a serious job search indefinitely, which is why I'm not going nowhere fast, I'm actually going nowhere rather slowly … If I was working my days in a coal mine (or slaughterhouse, tollbooth, door-to-door, etc.) I'd damn well be working on my resumé at night. Not so here.

But in the long run, sticking with the safe option of work that is not stimulating, but not horrible either, will kill you. Perhaps not literally (although the resultant alcoholism might) – but it will kill you inside. It is simply a slow, soft death, a sleepwalk to a retirement upon which all hopes have been pinned and which is therefore certain to disappoint.

The degree to which people are 'satisfied' with their jobs is a rich subject of academic study – and one filled with differences of opinion. There is at least agreement on a couple of points. First, workers in advanced economies express a fairly high degree of satisfaction with their jobs. Second, younger people generally express greater job dissatisfaction than their older colleagues. A number of explanations have been offered for this latter fact: that Generation X is simply more miserable generally; that the new 'insecurity' is negatively impacting the psyches of younger workers; or that younger workers simply tend to be in more junior, less exciting jobs.

But remember that satisfaction is relative. If your expectations are low you are more easily satisfied. It is most likely that younger workers have higher expectations of what their work will give them – and so are more likely to report dissatisfaction. Which, of course, is no bad thing. We *should* have high expectations of our work, we *should* be dissatisfied if they are not met, and we *should* (in that case) do something about it – which, as the higher turnover figures suggest, we increasingly are.

It's time to ratchet up our expectations of work. It's not surprising, given the recent history of attitudes towards work, that 'job satisfaction' has become the gold standard. But can you imagine being asked how things are with your lover and replying 'Well, it's satisfactory, thanks.' (Actually, come to think of it, a lot of English men probably can. That's another book.) It's difficult to be madly in satisfaction with someone. Few of us would settle for satisfaction in our romantic lives. Nor should we in our professional ones.

A culture of low expectations has been established around work. And it is a self-fulfilling prophecy. 'There is evidence of defeatism, of sticking with "your lot" rather than challenging the status quo,' say Laura Edwards and Nick Burkitt, who have examined the attitudes of low- and modestly paid workers. 'Enhancing the quality of people's working lives therefore means encouraging people, particularly those on low incomes, to expect it.'

The absence of meaningful work from so many people's lives is a direct result of our collective failure to demand it. 'We don't really expect work to give us much joy,' says Richard Leider. 'The Puritan ethic has convinced many of us that anything requiring hard work is valuable and anything that comes easily and does not require hard work is worth less.' Work, by definition, is supposed to be hard, soulless graft. That's why Terry Wogan says he's never done any work. Commentating and interviewing come naturally to him, so it can't be work. If we have a talent for something, we say 'it comes easily to us.' And for too long that has put it outside the world of work.

Contrast this attitude with the romantic notion that love in a personal relationship will dissolve all difficulties – exemplified in the stupid phrase 'love means never having to say you are sorry.' (In fact, love means exactly the opposite.) The assumption for too long has been that if it feels like work it can't be love and if it feels like love it can't be work. Both statements are dangerous distortions. Now, at last, we are starting to demand and find work that plays to our talents, which doesn't feel like work. Which might even feel like love.

Should I stay or should I go?

In his verse novel *The Golden Gate*, Vikram Seth describes two characters and how they relate to their work. One needs to go, the other to stay. John Brown is a computer programmer who makes a lot of money:

> … Silicon Valley
> Lures to ambition's ulcer alley
> Young graduates with siren screams
> of power and wealth beyond their dreams,
> Ejects the lax, and drives the driven,
> Burning their candles at both ends.
> Thus files take precedence over friends,
> Labor is lauded, leisure riven.
> John kneels bareheaded and unshod
> Before the Chip, a jealous God.

John's work is not part of his life. He has given up his life to his work in exchange for the by-products of it, especially money. His friend Janet Hayakawa, by contrast, has little money:

> She is a sculptor. Stress and pleasure
> For her thus perfectly combined,
> The boundaries of toil and leisure
> By definition ill-defined,
> Her worktime doubles as her playtime.

Which of these are you? For John, the value of work has been diminished to that of purely a means to some other end – money, status, power. It has become a corrosive presence in his life. It is time for John to go. If, on the other hand, you identify with Janet, if your work provides fulfilment, community and opportunities to learn, then it is worth staying – for the time being.

Not that work can always be wonderful, even for Janet. To pursue a job that brings no frustrations, no boredom, no conflict, no bad patches and no anxieties is like looking for a relationship that suffers from none of them, too – a wild goose chase. All jobs, and all relationships, contain difficulties. The question is whether they contain joy, too. As Wendell Berry says, 'All work contains drudgery. The issue is whether it contains meaning.'

Barbara Sher writes in the wonderfully titled *I Could Do Anything If I Only Knew What It Was* that there are two kinds of jobs, the 'toxic' job that simply poisons you and eats up your time (which you should dump) and the 'good' job that can be made great if you 'add your dream to it.' Now this is dangerously kooky-sounding stuff, but it is undeniably the case that one of the key factors in determining the quality of a job is what we bring to it. Gini says that 'work can bring out the divine as well as the demonic in us, raise us to creative heights, or drown us in despair. It all depends on the doer, what is being done, and why he is doing it.'

In the same way that we ask 'Is it me or them?' when a personal relationship is suffering, we have to look at whether it's really the job that's at fault, whether it's what we bring to it – or whether it is simply a case of not being right for each other. A series of poster ads for totaljobs.com highlights people who are out of sorts at work: a sheep shearer sitting in the middle of a string quartet, and a policeman with ballet shoes on. A clever taxi ad features a speech bubble coming from the driver window reading 'Trafalgar where?'; the company's tag line is 'In the wrong job?' Compatibility between you and your job is certainly critical to happiness. Some, like Ramesh, adore accounting; others would rather die than do it.

But the history of matching people to jobs is a chequered one. The idea, for example, that a computer test can tell a 16-year old which career is for them is laughable, if not downright dangerous. (When I undertook this exercise, the computer gave two rather different possible jobs top ranking: fighter pilot and museum curator. I suppose there's still time.) The point is that it takes time to figure out who we are, and therefore what work will express and expand our personalities – so 'career counselling' teenagers is tricky to pull off.

The recent vogue for workplace personality tests is dangerous too. While exercises like the famous Myers-Briggs psyhcometric text can be faintly useful for individuals, the idea that they can steer people into the right jobs – or determine their workplace behaviour – is scary. A company in Virginia had employees wear colour-coded badges indicating their Myers-Briggs personality type. The idea was that staff would communicate more effectively with someone they knew to be an 'introvert intuitive feeling perceiver' or an 'extrovert sensing thinking judger'. Scary.

Finding the right work is intensely personal and often mysterious to others. Science can help but it is mostly an art. Given the new salience of work in our lives, the real experts are the people who usually think about human relationships. Sarah Litvinoff, one of the UK's leading relationship counsellors, describes the following elements as the 'backbone of love' – and they can be applied as readily to your labours as to your lovers. So, with apologies to Litvinoff:

Liking: How much do you actually like your job? The initial excitement of landing it is one thing, but how about the day-to-day activity itself? Is it the kind of activity you would enjoy even if you were not being paid for it?

Humour: Being able to laugh is important in helping love of your job to last; if it's no fun, forget it. Humour also allows problems to be approached in proportion, so that minor niggles aren't taken too seriously.

Respect: Do you feel that you are treated with respect in your job? Equally, that you feel the work is worthwhile, that it commands respect is critical too.

Generosity: We've discussed gyms and dry-cleaners, and, of course, the important pay packet. You give generously of your time and talent. Your work should reward you generously in return.

Effort: Like all relationships, you do have to work at your job if it is to give you all you want. Striving to improve, to perform well, putting your heart and soul into it should improve how it feels. If not, it's time to say goodbye. Being down on your job can be a self-fulfilling prophecy.

If your work fails on one of the key backbone tests, it is time to start polishing the CV. If you ticked every one, congratulations. You have found work that fits you like a glove. Don't be shy: brag about it.

Spread the word: work can be great.

Tell me why you do like Mondays

There are plenty of us who do manage to find work that fits our talents and our lives, which stretches our minds, which is fun and important. There are plenty who love their jobs. But it's not socially acceptable, yet, to come out. There is a conspiracy of silence among those of you who simply adore your work. Perhaps you don't want to sound smug. Maybe you are afraid of offending friends who are in jobs they dislike. Whatever the reason, it's like a dirty secret.

Of course, those of us who admit to loving our work can face some stigma. Neil Kinnock, former leader of the Labour party once said of his colleague Gordon Brown, now British Chancellor, 'get him a hobby or a wife'. (As it happens, Mr Brown recently wed.) But why on earth did Kinnock say this? Because people who love their work – Brown is certainly one – often upset others, who may have simply stuck at their jobs and so see the joy that others get from work as a threat. It is the equivalent of people who don't like couples who are clearly madly in love because they are living proof that it is possible and so a reproach to those who have settled for less. So a person who just 'does the hours' and then goes home to stare at the television is supposed to be viewed in a more favourable light than someone who chooses to stay and work at a job that is intellectually challenging and fun.

There are some honourable exceptions to the depressing consensus, people who have owned up to their feelings. People like Sue, Ramesh, David, Marsha and Charlene. But the barriers to being honest can be high. Charlene says:

I am totally into doing a good job, doing it well. But I guess I play down my involvement with work. Why? I suppose the stigma of not seeming interesting, not well-rounded. But in fact, my work has taken me around the world, put me in contact with fascinating people and organisations. Still there is this guilt, this feeling that I should leave at 7pm. But why?

Marsha believes that attitudes towards work are changing more quickly than the public discourse about work. 'It is happening right now. There is real change happening in the way people think about work. Lots of them are quiet about it. It is now about giving people permission to change their work, and how they do it.'

People who love their work, who make their work the top priority in their lives, are not 'sad' or somehow 'missing out'. It is sad to stick in a job just because it happens to be the one you are in. It is sad to watch the clock every day, waiting to be released from a prison of your own making. And it is 'missing out' to be outside the growing group of people who derive enormous pleasure from what they do every working day of their lives.

Oliver Wendell Holmes says that 'most of us go to the grave with our music still inside us.' It's time to sing it out loud. It's time to come out of the closet. More of us love our work than are prepared to admit it – and we come from all walks of life. We have to create an unstoppable search for work that suits our needs, ignites our passion and fills our lives. If your job is empty, do something about it other than moan in the pub. Move on. And if you love your work, enjoy your enjoyment. Use your enthusiasm to win time sovereignty, relish the opportunities for personal growth. Legitimize love of work.

Once we've done that, we can hugely increase the demands we make of our work in return. We can rewrite the employment contract. Here's the deal: we love our work, but we have a few items we need in return. In fact, a whole new charter for work.

chapter nine
dream work

A job is not enough. A wage packet is not enough. We want more. Much more. Some of us are starting to get it – but only the very first shots have been fired in the workplace revolution. Crainer and Dearlove, in *Generation Entrepreneur*, capture the mood of the modern, powerful worker. 'This is the age of individual aspiration. We want. We need. We demand. We clamour. On Maslow's hierarchy of needs we're off the scale.'

We have exponentially rising expectations. And, increasingly, we are prepared to keep looking until they are met. Trade union leaders used to list the 'legitimate demands of the membership'. But they were pretty small beer: more money for less hours. The 'legitimate demands' of the modern worker are more extensive.

'It seems that employees have higher expectations than they used to,' says Margaret Malpas, director of Malpas training. 'It all leads to great expectations of wanting rather a lot and wanting it now. Because people want a lot they are prepared to push themselves harder to get it … they are prepared to move to get what they want from the right employer,' (*Guardian*, 13 November 2000).

What workers want might seem 'rather a lot' by historical standards. And those making greater demands sometimes get a sniffy response. They are sometimes seen as wanting 'too much', as being impatient and disloyal. But times have changed. Employers are not able to make us feel grateful for their kindness in giving us a job. The boot is firmly laced onto the other foot now. We used to know our place. Now we know our value.

Work is how we identify ourselves and where we learn. It is the passport to a community of friends and lovers. And as our work becomes more important to our quality of life in every dimension –

financial, social, emotional, physical – we have ratcheted up our expectations of it.

Our investment in work is high. The returns need to match.

The balance of power is shifting from companies (capital) to us (labour). This is especially true of 'knowledge workers' who carry the new means of production around on their shoulders. But it is true of millions of workers in the service sector too. The gap between the worker and the product, which Karl Marx identified, is narrowing fast. Signs of the new balance of power are everywhere, in pay structures and company beach houses, stock options and social events, in dress codes and dining-rooms.

Anyone with the required skills and knowledge is valuable to a firm. But a person who has found 'their work', the person whose work is a channel for their talents, who puts not just their brain but their heart and soul into their job, is gold dust. As such, they can demand the earth. And get it. We are simultaneously reclaiming our work and increasing our claim upon it. As Eva Bertram and Kenneth Sharpe argue in *The American Prospect*:

The politics of work is not just a struggle over distributive justice and meeting material needs. It is also a battle over the conditions within which we organise our time each day, much of which is spent on the job. How we structure those conditions will determine our prospects for building lives that are full, meaningful, and flourishing (11 September 2000).

In other words, the stakes just got raised. The old deal used to be that we, the workers, would exchange some time and effort for some money and a pension. This was a perfectly fair swap, but a very modest one – the equivalent of paying ten pence for a slightly cracked plate at a car boot sale.

Here's the new deal – we'll give you our passion, verve, enthusiasm, imagination, intelligence and 'that extra something' that comes from loving our work. But in exchange, we need a whole lot more than before. We have six demands:

We want to choose what we do.

We want to control it.

We want to reap the rewards of our own ideas.

We want money.

We want a superb working environment.

Oh, and we want to be able to jump ship whenever we feel like it.

This New Work Charter signals a profound shift in the relationship between work and worker. Historically, we have been forced into an occupational structure designed by others: the work maketh the man. Now we are demanding the right to create work in our image: the man maketh the work.

As Theodore Zeldin puts it, 'My question is not "How do we fit people to a career that will satisfy them?" but "How can we change the work they do so that it suits them?"' (*Fast Company*, December 2000).

The unfolding of the new, individual-driven, fluid, unstructured world of work will be the biggest social change of the early twenty-first century. It goes to the heart of how capitalist society is configured – and in whose interests. Early, industrial capitalism took work away from the worker. Now, as Western nations enter post-industrial economies, workers are taking it back. And once work is back in the hands – or head – of the worker, rather than the corporate HR department or 'careers adviser', everything changes. Some of those changes are becoming visible already. But be certain, you ain't seen nothing yet.

People power

Marianne Williamson's best-known poem was launched into global consciousness when Nelson Mandela quoted it in a post-apartheid speech. The opening reads:

> Our deepest fear
> is not that we are inadequate.
> Our deepest fear
> is that we are powerful beyond measure.

Williamson goes on to say that 'your playing small doesn't serve the world' and that those who allow their 'own light to shine' can serve as beacons to others. So it is in work: people who pursue their real ambitions at work and who love what they do should not be seen as belittling the work of others. They should be seen as role models, as pioneers.

People who work with skill and passion are now valuable 'beyond measure' – or at least beyond the usual measures of the labour market. James Carville was a little-known political strategist until he helped a certain Bill Clinton in 1991 and 1992. 'You pay for my head and I throw my heart in for free,' he said to his new boss. The rest, as they say, is history. Combine talent and the zeal of the person who has found their calling and you have a priceless package.

Sue delivers service above the norm to her customers – one reason she has been promoted after just months in her Safeway store:

A women came and asked me if we had any bread without wheat. I said I didn't know but I would found out. So I rang another branch and asked someone, and they said Bavarian White didn't have wheat. So I got a loaf and then went and found the woman and gave it to her. She was really pleased. And I learned something, too.

Alec Reed, founder and chairman of Reed plc, the temporary employment agency, has coined the term 'peoplism' to describe the new economic order, in which individual workers have become major players. Andy Westwood says that:

… peoplism is fundamentally about the rise in significance of individuals as factors of production … people are becoming more empowered within the labour market and are increasingly more aware of their own personal value … an individual can work their way around a labour market to their own … advantage.

Powerful workers who know their value can call the shots. They have high levels of security, not from a particular job, but from their knowledge of marketable skills in the broader labour market. Activism in the workplace is on the increase, even as trade unions continue their decline and fall. It is just that activism now takes the form of mobility rather than militancy. If we don't like the deal, we're not going to go to the union. We're just going to go.

The rules of the game are being rewritten. Terms which are commonly used in relation to work, such as 'security', 'risk', 'satisfaction', 'reward', 'loyalty' and 'career', are being redefined. Using old models can lead to wrong conclusions: like seeing high job turnover as a sign of insecurity, when it usually means the opposite; like seeing long hours as a sign of exploitation rather than enthusiasm; like seeing money as the principal reward for working, when people want much, much more and will sometimes trade money for it; like seeing staying with a firm as a sign of 'loyalty', when it is often a sign of disloyalty to yourself and your dreams.

It can all look confusing, as Westwood points out:

Peoplism is an aggregation of different and sometimes contradictory economic and social factors that fundamentally changes the position of individuals within society and the world of work. It is a combination of labour market confidence and job insecurity; corporate responsibility and individual risk; entrepreneurialism and stakeholding.

We have already seen, particularly in Chapter Four, how some companies are responding to the new balance of power, offering a wider range of services to sought-after staff. But they are not doing enough for enough of us.

Raising our sights

If work is uninspiring our lives lack inspiration too. Al Gini says that 'too many of us feel that our lives as workers have been a failure because work has failed to give us what we need.'

More and more of us are deriving enormous pleasure from our work – and being rewarded for our labours of love. This is clearly good news. But it also throws into sharper relief the existence of jobs which dilute the humanity of the worker. Gini says that the 'failure of work' can be manifested in:

… diminished self-esteem, toil without dignity … petty bureaucratic politics, the purposelessness of many of our tasks, the gnawing lack of creativity, fulfilment, and genuine sense of involvement on the job, the absence of autonomy, the increasing sense of isolation, excessive competitiveness, ineffective and inept leadership, physical and psychological enervation…

The good news is that there aren't many people working in these conditions. The bad news is that there are any at all. The relentlessly negative messages about work that continue to the present day have allowed dismal work to continue. If our expectations about work are low then there's a good chance they'll be met. Like our politicians, we get the work we deserve. And up until now we have not seen ourselves as especially deserving.

Of course, the demand for more meaning from our work is causing difficulties and some angst. Life was easier when we all settled for less, but only in the sense of the ease of the French peasantry before 1789. Work is having to accommodate new and rapidly rising demands for fulfilment and reward. But it's about time. Enough is enough. Our sights are raised. Revolution is in the air.

Institutions which might be expected to lead the charge for better work – especially trade unions and centre-left political parties – remain, by and large, stuck playing the old work-is-bad record. For them, fighting on behalf of workers has essentially meant trying to get as much money for as little effort as possible. This was absolutely the right strategy in the industrial era, but is absolutely inappropriate for today's workers. But unions have found it hard to shake off the legacy of the 'more money for less time' years, which were, after all, their heyday.

As Reg Theriault explains:

… trade unions and their leadership have no programs or ideology of their own … After wage increases and fringe benefits, trade unions have exhausted their claim on the world we live in … Retiring earlier is great. So is another week off sometime during the summer. And more money – we all know what to do with *that*. But what about all those days of our years between the ages roughly of twenty and sixty-five, the longest and most significant period of our lives?

So it's up to us. Businesses know the mood is shifting, and are beginning to change their spots, because talented people who put their hearts and souls into their work are not just the happiest workers around: they are the most valuable too.

The New Work Charter

We know that companies need us more than we need companies.
And we are a demanding bunch. Here's what the new heart-and-
soul worker wants. Here's the six-point New Work Charter.

Suits you

Workers have traditionally been fitted to their work. The best they
could hope for was to be matched with careers that would make use
of their skills. At the peak of worker control, time-and-management
studies attempted to turn people into parts of an efficient machine;
Frederick Taylor wanted to measure, automate, segregate and control
workers. But now we want to be able to fit the work to our needs and
desires.

We want tailor-made jobs, not Taylor-made ones.

Charles Handy says that firms now need to 'offer opportunities
rather than jobs – a creative space'. John Knell agrees that
employment offerings will have to be cut to fit the worker. 'While
highly specific and differentiated contracts are a feature of nearly all
markets, they are not yet commonplace in the labour market. They
are about to become so for knowledge workers.'

In order to attract and retain passionate, highly skilled staff – the
precious metals of the new economy – companies have to provide
the benefits of self-employment in-house. Robert Reich, the former
US Secretary of Labor, says that successful firms will 'offer many of
the advantages of free agency; flexibility in how, when and where
you work; compensation linked to what you contribute; freedom to
move from project to project. They are the enterprises of the future.'

Some of us want lots of strategic input but are not interested in management; some of us like to work regular hours behind a desk, while others want to work in the garden on Sundays; some of us like to work in teams, others are loners. And so on. Rather than trying to ram square pegs into round holes, companies have to square the holes.

The individual desire for a made-to-measure job rather than an off-the-peg number coincides with a commercial need for greater flexibility. Given the speed of market change, it's hard for companies to draw up detailed job descriptions that can be signed up to by both sides as a fixed set of expectations.

Management experts Hammer and Champy describe the needs of business:

For multi-dimensional and changing jobs, companies don't need people to fill a slot, because the slot will be only roughly defined. Companies need people who can figure out what the job takes and do it, people who can create the slot that fits them. Moreover, the slot will keep changing.

The days of the job description are numbered. This is good news, because fewer and fewer of us are prepared to be slot-fillers. We want work that surprises and challenges us, that allows for digression, new projects, new people. Incidentally, the New Work Charter also means the abolition of grades and bands. Some organizations still function like secondary schools, putting people into certain 'sets', with associated pay and other rewards. In some cases, someone who has pulled off a seriously successful project can't be properly rewarded because they are only a Band B or whatever.

The *Brave New World* division of workers into Alphas, Betas and so on is anathema to heart-and-soul workers. Grading systems are for the kind of people who keep all their till receipts. They are not for us. Can you imagine someone saying to Georges Seurat, 'These pictures are very nice, and the dots are particularly interesting, but you are only a Grade Five, you know, and rather young. You have to be a Grade Three before we can exhibit anything. Sorry. But remember: good things come to he who waits!'?

Banded bureaucracy drives passionate people away. They don't want to be sorted, labelled and put in their place. They don't care too much for rules either.They want to bring their dogs to work, fine. Wear leather jackets, fine. Wander off without notice, fine. Rules and regulations are the enemies of passion, adventure and creativity. Once a couple starts having 'rules' in their relationship you know they've had it. It's the same with jobs and people who love their work. Rules ruin.

Values, by contrast, are vital. Workers who are sure of their own values want to be sure of the values of the firm they sign up to. Their work is the most important act of self-expression in their lives. As such, it has to send the right message. They want to feel good about what they do. 'What you value is unmistakably reflected in precisely how you spend your time,' Tom Peters reminds us.

Controlling passions

Needless to say, however good a place it is, we get to decide when and whether to turn up. Passionate workers want time sovereignty, as discussed in Chapter Six. The work does not dictate our hours, we do. This is the second Charter demand.

It can be hard for some companies to meet the demand for time sovereignty. Crainer and Dearlove say that 'old style managers hate not seeing their people. They remain addicted to treating people as if they were at school instead of telling them to go away and do something as they would at university.'

Newsflash … newsflash … they are not 'your people' any more. And if you try to push them into antiquated working patterns they will up sticks and leave. People who get time sovereignty are much more likely to love their work, and people who love their work are going to take time sovereignty for granted.

Elizabeth Perle McKenna, who writes eloquently and mostly wrongly against work in *When Work Doesn't Work Anymore*, makes an admission about her experience of writing the book. 'I had enjoyed control over what I was producing. I assigned my own tasks, decided what to do when, and what might be the best way of doing it … I was being paid to do this. The realisation stunned me. I love my work; it works for me.'

That Perle McKenna should be 'stunned' is a measure of the damage done to the idea and expectation of meaningful work. Control and choice are the critical ingredients of any relationship of value. Few of us would expect an arranged marriage to a dictator to be a happy one. Yet that is the model of work we are still struggling to abandon.

Requests for flexible working sometimes gets wrapped up with a desire to 'downshift'. But control over our working time is not a plea for idleness, or less work. Indeed the evidence is that work freely given is more plentiful than work done by the clock. We are prepared to invest a great deal of time, energy and talent in our work – but on our terms.

There may be some people who want to slow down a little, who want to drop out of a competitive worklife which – speaking volumes about our attitudes – we dub a 'rat race'. These are the people who enviously watch *The Good Life*, a 1970s sitcom about a couple who live in suburban self-sufficiency with a large vegetable garden and various contraptions.

But 'the good life' is the dull life. For all the collective nostalgia for a 'slower pace of life', being busy is good. The new malaise is supposed to be 'hurry sickness'. City-dwellers are taught to long for the happier, more serene life of the countryside. But the 'pace' of modern life is a reflection of the broadening range of activities we want to engage in, rather than a sign of being overstretched.

Robert Levine, in *A Geography of Time*, points out that it is tempting to assume that slow is good and quick is bad, but then proves the opposite. 'In all pace-of-life experiments, people in faster places were more likely to be satisfied with their lives.' We want to be busy, we want full lives. We want to work hard, sometimes very hard. Not because we are being forced to, but because we want to. Because it is more fun and more satisfying than the alternatives.

Whose idea was this? (clue: mine)
David Shaw, who manages a hedge fund, always tries to invest in any bright ideas any of his staff come up with. But he wasn't always like this. He learned the hard way. A few years back he said a cheery and indulgent farewell to a staff member who was leaving to pursue an idea for a new dot.com company. The employee, Jeff Bezos, called his fledging firm Amazon.com.

Ideas are the capital of the new economy and for a while companies were able to extract and exploit their employees' brainpower. Now we've wised up. Intellectual property is a slippery beast; it is easy for staff to work on a killer idea and use it to start up a competitor firm rather than give it to the boss. Indeed, it often makes more financial sense to go solo. 'Employers have rightly come to see their employees as potential competitors.'

Control over our own intellectual property is the third demand in the New Work Charter. Firms have to find ways of allowing talented workers access to the profits flowing from the originality of their thinking. Workers want to turn intellectual capital into financial capital – not just hand it over to the firm.

Some companies draw up fiercely complex contracts attempting to assert copyright over any ideas springing from their employees' heads. And 'non-compete' clauses are common in industries such as PR and advertising. But these sticks rarely work. Proving that someone had an idea on 'work time' is like proving that your partner was unfaithful to you in a dream: impossible and pointless.

Instead, firms have to invest in our ideas and share the profits. As Knell puts it, 'back my idea or watch my back.' A number of firms, such as Accenture and IBM, have established in-house venture capital funds and set up joint ventures with their own employees. These are the new employment deals. As the European Head of AC Ventures says, 'We'd rather our staff went to start-ups we're investing in than those we are not.'

As well as support for and financial payback from our ideas we want space in which to develop them. Too much 'work' time is spent in useless meetings. Bruce Mau's design company usefully differentiates between 'meetings', which deal as quickly as possible with mundane matters, and 'workings', which are brainstorming sessions, strategy planning, meetings of minds. The rise in popularity of 'bullshit bingo' – in which players tick off well-worn management clichés uttered during meetings until someone has a 'full house' – shows the depths to which the value of work time has sunk.

Smohalla, a chief of the Nez Percé American Indian tribe, said, 'My young men shall never work. Men who work cannot dream, and wisdom comes in dreams.' You can sort of see his point. But work without dreams is a soulless activity. Today, men and women who work not only want the space to dream, they need it if they are to create the ideas which mean the difference between failure and success. We work, perchance to dream.

Love can buy you money

If I love my work, I want to be well-rewarded. The idea that a 'labour of love' comes cheap is history. It used to be the case that people were prepared to choose between an unfulfilling job that paid for the weekend house and a meaningful job that paid badly. Not any more. Salaries in the charitable sector have been rising rapidly in recent years. The artificial division between interesting work that paid badly and bad work that paid well was a legacy of a world view that suggested work could not both provide meaning and be profitable. If we manage to find work that draws upon our natural talents, and in which we invest our brains and souls, we should be rewarded handsomely. This is not an either/or equation.

We don't work for the money any more – that was so Eighties – but that doesn't mean we don't want it. We want lots of it. The fourth Charter demand is money – cash, shares, options, pensions, bonuses, golden hellos. The works. John Harrison, the man who made the world's first accurate watches, clearly loved his work. The 19 years it took him to build the world-changing H3 model were years of driven vocation. And he was fêted as a genius. Did he settle for that? No. He rightly fought to get the £20,000 prize offered by the British Parliament, which rivals were trying to snatch. Building time-pieces was Harrison's calling, by all accounts, a true labour of love. But that didn't diminish his desire for financial reward too.

Salaries have risen in an effort to keep pace with the growing demand to be rewarded for passion and imagination. This is especially true in 'knowledge industries' where high-quality, engaged staff are vital. Large law firms in Silicon Valley have pushed up salaries by 30–40 per cent across the board to try to halt the dot.com desertions. Accenture in the UK is offering graduates a £10,000 'golden hello'.

Performance-related pay and bonus schemes have all flourished, and rightly so. People who put their all into their work should be better paid than the jobsworth who does the minimum required. Two-thirds of British firms now have some sort of performance-based system, up from a third just a couple of years ago. Many are piecemeal – but it represents the beginning of a movement to pay for passion rather than presence.

Westwood points out that wage inequalities are increasing not only between occupations, but within occupations too. 'It would appear that in the new economy workers are being rewarded for that "extra something",' he says. 'The indefinable human element people bring to the labour market whatever their position in the job hierarchy.' About time, too. That 'extra something' comes from our passion for the job – which certainly should be rewarded.

Last, but not least, we want a slice of the company. Stock options and shares are, according to Professor Manuel Castells, chief chronicler of the network economy, the 'currency of the new economy'. If you want talented, heart-and-soul workers to stick around, giving them a stake in the firm is a useful dab of glue. Nor is this restricted to those at the top of the tree: there are one million workers in the UK who belong to share-ownership schemes. Staff at supermarket chain ASDA made up to £52,000 each in 2000 from investments in the company's share saving scheme.

And it works for firms too. Sales, performance and employment are all shown to rise faster in companies which introduce employee share-ownership schemes. Reich explains. 'If you want talent to work for your organisation with the enthusiasm that comes with ownership, then you have to trade equity for it.'

The relationship used to be so simple: workers clocked on, firms coughed up. Now workers, holding the means of production in their heads, are working with enthusiasm, ambition and with themselves nominated as chief beneficiaries. We want good salaries, but we also want extra for the something extra that we know we bring. And we want a share of the share price action too, if we are to help push it up for you.

But that's not all. Don't think for a second that any of this will buy you our loyalty. We are loyal only to our work, not to a specific job or firm. In fact, we don't want to stay a minute longer than necessary.

Exit all areas
A recent article in *US News and World Report* was titled 'Why It Pays to Quit' and further explained 'Loyalty, shmoyalty. In today's

frenzied job market, staying put gets you nowhere. Walking out gets you ahead.'

Of course it's not true that walking out necessarily gets you ahead. Some people jump from frying pan to fire. But it's true that having the power to walk out does.

Loyalty is low – workers consistently say they will move for better opportunities. This is good news. Loyalty to a firm that is offering dull work in a depressing environment would be a sign of mental instability and/or low self-esteem, like loyalty to an abusive partner. The power of exit is critical and is the fifth demand of the New Work Charter. Firms have to consciously make us vulnerable to being poached and live with a decision on our part to (literally) part company. Companies have to live with the near-certainty of our imminent departure as the price for having us around at all.

Bruce Pasternack, a management writer, describes this as a 'New People's Partnership', in which the company 'assumes responsibility for investing in the employee and providing work that makes the individual "employable" in the marketplace'. In other words, firms have to give us our departure tickets. He goes on to say that the company:

… must support employees in identifying career opportunities inside *and outside* the company, helping them to build a customised career path. In this environment, there is no stigma attached to looking for a new job …

If you want me, set me free. Make me a prized commodity.

If you want me, set me free. Make me a prized commodity. Treat poaching as a source of pride. That means constant learning activities. If you give me valuable skills, I'm more likely to stick around, for a while at least. Janice Brown, a training expert, says, 'We review the position every six months … it is quite unusual for someone to leave if they are looking forward to the next course,' (*Observer*, 26 November 2000).

But learning has to come not just from courses but from colleagues too (see Chapter Three). This means creating a culture of learning within the organization and, crucially, ensuring that those with the skills and knowledge are sharing them. Bob Garratt, in *The Learning Organisation*, argues that a learning organization can only begin to take shape if the people with the skills and knowledge are aware of their abilities and are sharing them with colleagues. These people, the mentors of the learning company, have what Garratt dubs 'conscious competence'. These are the ones to cultivate.

They contrast with those with 'conscious incompetence' (who know they're no good), 'unconscious competence' (good but don't know or share it) and – most dangerous and familiar of all – 'unconscious incompetence' (hopeless but think they're good). These last ones are the people to keep away from your stars.

Exit power in the modern labour market means access to networks, to other potential employers or partners. Some companies force visitors to sign 'don't recruit' agreements for fear of losing staff. This is short-sighted.

Smart, enthusiastic, heart-and-soul workers won't work unless they are certain of access to future employment opportunities. Trying to hide them away won't work. Companies simply have to learn to lose people but stay in touch. As Knell says, 'Firms will have to get better at tracking the most talented people they have worked with. Smart companies will not only have to get better at their employment relations, but also their alumni relations.'

Talent is mobile. Firms have to live with that. It may be that someone will leave but return at a later stage, or become a client or supplier, or enter into a new partnership. Firms that want heart-and-soul workers have to become better at 'letting people go' – in the proper sense of the term.

Environmental management
Workers who live to work are not gluttons for punishment. They are the opposite. They are utterly unforgiving of an environment that makes them feel less than great. And it has to feel good for them to stay for long. Lots of the goodies discussed in Chapters Four and Five (gyms and crèches and bars and friends and lovers) are not perks – they are part of the basic package.

Fun and work often feel like mutually exclusive categories. But today's workers are rejecting the distinction. They want – and get –

the money and the fun. A great environment – physical, intellectual and social – is the last, but certainly not least, item on the New Work Charter.

George Colony, CEO of Forrester, a technology research firm, has kept his turnover of staff down to 20 per cent a year, very low by dot.com standards. 'If we keep people for five or six years it's a big win for us,' he says. 'We're living in a world where every employee is a free agent. People can get money anywhere. Why do people stay in one place? It comes down to a company's environment,' (*Fast Company*, December 2000).

The old working model was based on deferred gratification. Workers tolerated the work because it funded their lives after five and their retirement after 65. If you served your time you were rewarded with a promotion and then a pension. This is not how we think about work now.

Audrey Collin writes that 'the focus of career could shift from constructing the future in primarily temporal terms (time-line, trajectory, directional continuity) to more spatial terms (horizontal, non-directional continuity)'. Lash and Urry describe this as 'the future dissolving into the present'.

In other words, gratification has to be instant. We still want all the good things, but not to be forced to wait for them. The career as an exercise in delayed gratification is dead. No one wants to be a time-server now. Jam today.

The need to attract people to work is most acute in sectors where people not only have the power to work elsewhere, they have enough money not to work at all. Microsoft has made many of its employees very wealthy, which means they have to work harder to hang on to them. The challenge, say Microsoft HR people, is not people ringing in sick. It is people ringing in rich.

CISCO has the same problems, but also manages to hang on to people by providing work that stimulates and challenges. Once money is taken out of the equation as a critical factor, the environment is key. 'Plenty of people could buy their own Hawaiian islands,' says Peter Clarke, a CISCO business development director. 'But we love coming to work. I've got a small cottage and I sometimes think to myself that it'd be nice to go and hang out there. But what would I do? After three months I'd be going nuts,' (*Guardian*, 21 November 2000).

This, then, is the sixth Charter demand of work: that its environment is enticing enough that we would keep going even if it made us rich enough not to (which we hope it does). That is mostly about the content of the work, but also about the social environment – and of course the range of services that are available. Dry-cleaning, just to pick a random example. OK, so it's not random. Just in case the message hasn't got through: we don't like doing laundry.

The New Work Charter is ambitious. It will remain utopian until we collectively admit the central importance of work in our lives and stop tolerating work that does not give us a fair exchange for our labour.

As a society we have reached a critical point in our relationship to work. People want to work more than ever before, although not, by and large, at their current jobs. Our expectations of what we want from work have leapt upwards, along with our willingness to devote ourselves to work that we love. Work *is* getting much better – but not fast enough. We want more. And we want it now.